I0203432

Anywhere But

Here

Written by: Patty Mac

Copyright 2013, All Rights Reserved

Table of Contents

Prologue

ANYWHERE BUT HERE is loosely-based on a true story of survival for a young girl named Lexis. She is trapped by her mother's abuse and she feels doomed to Hell by the convictions of the religion she grew up with. In addition, she is indoctrinated by her stepfather's perverse ideas of God. She does however inherit her Granny's gift of second sight (clairvoyance), which conflicts dramatically with her religious upbringing.

She faces the wrath of her mother's scorn and abuse every day. Granny Millie's love provides Lexis with the strength to go on to escape the circumstances of her life.

Her story is one of despair, hope and fear yet with a strength of courage and hope that defied the odds.

Desperate to run away from the life she has been born into, her soul craves for freedom. She will do anything to escape so that she can be ANYWHERE BUT HERE.

***

CHAPTER 1

Granny Milly

My Granny Milly was a very strict woman. She had a commanding presence when she walked into any room. You could hear a pin drop as people hung on to her every word. It wasn't just the way she looked since Granny Milly was short in stature, with her long hair always pulled back in a tight, neat bun on the top of her head and bobby pins keeping every single hair in place.

She always wore a flowered dress, with a bib apron covering her ample bosom. Most times her face had a small patch of flour somewhere, usually on her cheek. Her brown skin felt like leather to the touch and she always smelled of home-baked cookies and bread even when she wasn't in the kitchen baking. There was always a twinkle in her eyes that seemed to look right into and through your very soul.

She was the type of woman that made all children afraid to look directly into her eyes not because she was mean but because she seemed to know exactly what you were thinking or what you were going to ask her before the words could come out of your mouth. While she wasn't exactly what I would call emotional by any means, she did show a lot of compassion for so many people in the little towns that lined the coast of the island that we all lived on. Trying to help as many people as she could in the only way she really knew how, cooking and baking from morning till night for all to come fill their bellies. She would send out food to the neighboring towns to a hard-done-by family who couldn't afford to feed their children that week for whatever reason.

Most of the towns were permanently poverty stricken. Either you fished lobster or you worked in the coal mine. Either one was a very dangerous way to make a living. So many times as a child, I remember the flags flying at half-mast because the cold Atlantic Ocean had taken another husband from his wife and another father from his children. It always seemed to be the ocean stealing souls. They lost their lives fishing through the rough coastal waters, always worried about getting enough stamps for their pogie (a term we used for unemployment insurance) so they could feed their families for the winter.

I remember the waves crashing so high some days with the wind and the rain, the waves would touch the cliff tops of the shore (at least 15 feet high). When the storms hit all the mines that ran under the island (which stretched for miles into the ocean) the pressure would cause the walls to collapse and flood trapping the miners with no way to escape. They were doomed to a dark watery grave most times, there was no way to even retrieve their bodies so that section of the mine would be shut down and another section opened up and the coal mining would continue as if nothing had ever happened

Our little island was only 3981 square miles around. It was called Cape Breton Island by the French, why I'm not quite sure. Cape Breton Island is lined with coastal towns with most people living off and on the land. Mining was the main income source in the small town where I was from, called Glace Bay named by the French in the 1720's because of the sea ice that filled the ocean every winter. Other towns and villages lived off farming and fishing. Lobster was a big money maker for the fishermen in the next town over. Although to me it seemed like no one had much money those days not that I can remember anyways.

I had learned through the history teachings in my school that at one point our island was actually physically attached to the mainland of Nova Scotia but was separated after millions of years of continental drift.

Now it is artificially connected to the mainland of Nova Scotia by a long rock-filled strip called the Canso Causeway.

In the very center of the island sits one of the world's largest salt water lakes named the Bras d'Or lakes by the French, signifying "arms of gold".

Predominantly trees, lakes, mountains and valleys, Cape Breton is full of beauty for all eyes to see from the outside world. What happens in the small towns behind those closed doors that the outside world didn't see and no one ever talked about was another issue. The "family shame" it was called by so many of us, our family had a lot of shame that we kept hidden for many years, sometimes beyond our death. Cape Breton was not only separated to the mainland by water but by a language barrier and a culture so very different from the outside world. We even developed our own dictionary and language over the years, called the mudder tongue because of the strong accents and different words our people used. Mother was actually pronounced "mudder" and when you couldn't find a name for something it was called a "queer ma jigger". Saying to someone, *"Go get me the queer ma jigger or the whatcha ma call It."* were common terms although I won't focus on them too much in my story.

So back to the story at hand.

A Beating to Remember

I remember after one particular beating from my mother when we went for our weekly Sunday visit. The drive there always seemed to take an eternity with us 4 kids squashed into the back of our old red car. The car belonged to my stepfather George. My mother had moved in with him the minute she left my father, or so it seemed to me. It was his car she drove, his house we lived in and his family we were surrounded by on a daily basis.

Ann was my younger sister by 3 years; then there was Vin who was 11 months older than me, and Joe who was 11 months younger than me. Mother always said that by the time she was pregnant with Ann she was so tired of having kids that she didn't even bother to pick out a name for her, so she named her after some nurse that worked in the hospital. That's how Ann got her name when she was born. Ann was sitting uncomfortably on the floor with an old piece of tin riveted over a rusty hole in the floor of the car as the only thing keeping her from falling onto the road to her death.

The salt in the air from the ocean rotted everything; your cars, your homes and whatever else it got its grasp on. Every house was made of painted shingles (if you were lucky enough to be able to afford paint). Otherwise, the neighbors would gather up all their leftover gallons and mix them together not caring what color it created as long as it saved the remaining shingles. People did their own work on their cars. With a rivet gun and tin picked from the dump that would hold the car together through another long winter. Every spring we would take a-trip to the dump, scrounging like the rest of the town looking for pieces of tin and wood to fix what the winter of that year had rotted.

Granny Milly lived in the next town, about a 30 minute drive of nothingness except for trees and old rundown houses. You rarely ever saw a car on the road. After all it was Sunday, a day when everyone went to church then home to spend the day with their families.

The car was always so quiet on the half hour drive to Granny Millie's. The 4 of us were afraid to make a sound for fear of mother's unknown temperament and often violently rageful reactions. It usually didn't take much to set her off. She would often say, *"Let me hear one peep from you kids and look out!"* before we even got into the car. No matter how squashed you were or who was sitting on whose leg, you never dared to complain because mother might fly into one of her rages pulling over to the side of the road, dragging you out of the car and then God only knows what would happen, usually mother losing all control of her emotions and giving us the beating of our lives yelling the whole time we were getting what she swore we deserved.

In the uncomfortable silence of the car all I had was nothing but time – time to think. Thinking about a way to escape this horrible life I had been born into and held hostage in.

My mind wandered to Granny Milly as I wondered if she would even notice what was wrong with me that Sunday. If she did notice would she say anything? I was terrified at the thought that she might. She wasn't one to ever hold anything back.

In my family (and most of the families in our small town) what happened behind closed doors, stayed behind closed doors. Everything was always such a huge secret. Don't get me wrong, people would whisper and speculate about the goings on in other people's homes but nothing was ever said out loud. That's just the way it was. The odd time when something came to light about someone in the community, it was completely denied or brushed off like it was nothing of importance. Someone beating his or her wife would deny it. Someone hurting his or her child denied it. You could witness it with your own eyes, or hear it with your own ears, but it was always kept secret. It was like a massive conspiracy.

As we pulled up to the old 3 story run-down house, fear gripped me as I wondered what I would say to her if she asked. Quickly, it was forgotten as we drove up the long dirt lane to her house and I could see all of my cousins playing in the old apple tree in the front yard.

Granny's house was huge, with a cold cellar in the basement. It was supposed to be gray in color, but most of the paint was peeling - or cracking - showing the bare rotting wood shingles underneath. The rotted shingles were replaced once a year in the spring after the long cold winter.

There were old storm windows that covered every single window in the house to keep out the bitter cold and wind. You knew it was a sure sign of spring when they were taken down to let the glorious sunshine through. It had bedrooms on every floor, each one covered in old brown wallboard and burgundy shag -type carpet (it was the 70's!). This to best accommodates all of her kids. Granny had 15 kids of her own! They always seemed to have their friends hanging around the old house with them, but granny never seemed to mind making room for more.

No Rest for a Wicked

No sooner than you opened the door to the porch, a delicious aroma from whatever granny was cooking or baking hit your nostrils right away before you even reached the kitchen door.

Granny always seemed to be hovering over the stove cooking or baking something. She noticed the huge cut above my eye the minute I looked at her. *"What happened, my child?"* she asked as soon as my mother was out of earshot. *"I fell into the cupboard door"* I told her. *"Is she hitting you? Because if she is, so help me..."* Granny vowed. *"No, she's not. I swear!"* I said, choking back the tears. Funny, even at that young age, I had learned not to trust anyone, even the person I loved the most in the whole world. *"You wait till your mother goes over to visit Granny Demeyer. I have something to talk to you about."* she said.

Instantly, I was afraid. I really wasn't sure why my stomach felt like it had jumped into my throat the minute I heard those words. It wasn't until years later, in my early 20's, that I was finally able to figure out why.

That feeling of fear stemmed from mother. In my experience when she needed to "talk" to any of us kids that usually meant we were going to get the tar beat out of us for something we did or didn't do. There was no reasoning with mother once she got something in her mind. When she left us alone with George it was the worst. A knot would form in the pit of my stomach the minute I knew she was leaving and it would grow bigger and bigger as each moment passed and I waited for her rage-filled return. It comes to mind now when I think back on those days, you see mother always seemed to need something or someone to be angry at. Usually it was me who took the brunt of her anger.

She would walk through the door with that look of madness in her eyes and the fear would rise up inside of me and run through me from head to toe.

"Go upstairs I need to talk to you", was all she would say, of course there was never any talking. Each beating we received as a consequence of her leaving us alone with George was just a repeat of the last in a vicious cycle.

You see George was in the habit of preaching fire and brimstone to us kids and anyone else who would listen, whilst he was touching both me and my sister Ann in the most inappropriate places. Mother would rage every frustration she ever had in her life out on the children she had brought into this world, the ones that she was supposed to love and care for. Leaving us home alone with George was just as good of an excuse as any for her rage.

"I probably won't be allowed." I told her. I think it was more out of fear of what she had to talk to me about, than the fear of asking to stay and getting a good beating when I got home.

Granny made me my favorite –mushroom soup -made with real cows' milk, surrounded by 2 pieces of warm toast, all laid on a plate like I was a princess. She asked me several more times what had happened, then gave up. I thought the whole thing had been forgotten.

10

My mother came back from visiting her brother. He lived in the trailer right across the lane from Granny Milly with his wife and 3 small kids. Granny asked mother if I could go pick some blueberries for her. I thought that was her reason for wanting me to stay.

"Why do you need her to pick the berries for you, when you got all the kids around here to do it?" was mother's angry reply.

"Well," said Granny (boy was she a quick thinker) *"I have orders for 20 pies by tomorrow morning, and Minny and Cat are so tired from picking all day yesterday and this morning."*

Minny and Cat were my aunts. Minny was just a few months older than me where Cat was well over a year and a half older. Minny and I were very close, but Cat and I – not so much. I swear I held my breath for the whole conversation. I was never allowed to stay anywhere without my mother being within earshot! Finally, after what seemed like an eternity, my mother finally said yes. If it weren't for the fear of the beating I would get, I would have jumped up and hugged my Granny so hard, I probably would have choked her.

The minute mother was out of the driveway; my Granny kicked all the other kids out of the old house, and sat me down for a long talk.

"You know," she said, *"You're my first granddaughter. I love you very much, and you are very special to me. But your mother, she has problems, and to be honest, I am not even sure what they are. A couple of years ago when you were about two years old, I took a surprise visit down to your mother's house. I hadn't seen any of you kids in about two weeks, and I was very worried. I was quite surprised when I got there and your mother didn't open the door for me. Finally, I told her if she didn't open the door, I would be calling the police to see if you kids were okay. What I saw was something*

I will never forget as long as I live. There you were, your face so swollen. I wasn't even sure if it was you at first. You were so afraid."

"I was so mad! I really wanted to strangle your mother" granny said, *"but instead I calmly asked her what had happened to you. She replied that you had fallen down the stairs. The cellar door was opened and you went right through to the bottom. I asked her if she had taken you to the hospital. She answered yes. I then asked your father, but he swore up and down he wasn't there. So I gave you kids your treats and left. I drove straight to the hospital to see if you had actually been there. Something told me your mother was lying. Anyway, I checked with them. They had no records of any child falling into a cellar from the top of the stairs. I headed straight back to your mother's.*

This time I didn't wait for her to tell me I couldn't come in. I just busted through the door and proceeded to pick you up to take you home with me. It was a bitter fight, but in the end, she admitted to losing her temper and beating you. I told her at that point, that if I ever saw another bruise on you, I wouldn't hesitate to have her thrown in jail, no matter what I had to tell the police. She swore I never would see you bruised again, and I haven't up until today, so if there is anything you need to tell me Lexis, please do, because I only want to help you".

I was so shocked by what I had just heard, all I could do was sit on her lap and cry.

Did I tell her? Well, yes I did, and to be quite honest with you, I really don't think I regretted one word of the story I was about to tell. I felt like I sat on her lap for an eternity, feeling her leathery skin brush up against my cheek as she kissed away my tears, but I'm sure it was only about 20 minutes. But in that time, I felt more love and security than I ever felt in my short life. So as afraid as I was of the consequences, I decided to open up to her, my Granny, my guardian angel; sent here to let me know that in this big cruel world, there is always someone out there who loves you unconditionally. You just have to let go and trust.

It was really hard at first but once the words started coming they seemed like they would never stop. *"Granny,"* I sobbed, *"Granny, she hates me."*

God, how I wanted to tell her how I thought I hated her too, but the shame of those unnatural feelings wouldn't let me speak them.

"Why child, would you ever say such a thing?" she asked. *"She beats me. Vin and Joe get to tell her they love her every night and she kisses them and tells them she loves them back. But when Ann or I call her into our room to get a kiss, she slaps us. Then she leaves our room all mad and stuff, saying under her breath how she hates us, and why did she ever have to be cursed with girls like us."*

By this time I was sobbing so uncontrollably, that I made a mad dash for the bathroom, vomiting across the spotlessly clean black and white tile. After I had finished being sick, I quickly grabbed a towel from under the sink to clean up my mess, fearing the worst, that those safe precious moments with my Granny were lost forever. To my surprise, Granny shooed me from the bathroom. When I opened the bathroom door, the mess was cleaned. Not a word was said about it.

"So child, tell me what really happened" she said.

So I did. *"Well"* I said, *"George who was my stepfather worked at the forum or the skating rink as it was called back then. Rarely did we get to go skating there though but when we did it always seemed to be the highlight of my life. George was a lot older then mother by like 20 years I think. I really can't remember when they first got together I was real young I guess. George had a bottle of Pepsi in the fridge. I guess when he went to get it, half of it was gone. So he said "Woman, (that's what he called my mother) one of these kids drank my Pepsi."*

You see, the way us 4 kids were raised was that George worked every day to raise the 4 bastards that weren't his, so we were supposed to be eternally grateful. He got special food like Pepsi, real milk, and meat pies bought from the grocery store. Funny, we all use to sit around the stairs when he was eating one of those fancy meat pies, just waiting, hoping he would be full so he would offer one of us the leftover crust. That was the only time we would volunteer to sit on the stairs since Mother sometimes used this as a form of punishment. There would be no fidgeting or moving and only 2 toilet breaks for the day.

Granny Milly would also use sitting on the stairs as a form of punishment but it never seemed to be as severe. A perfect example of this was when Granny Milly had grounded one of my uncles to the stairs. He tied a long white string around the stair railing and then around his waist and proceeded to walk around the living room. Granny asked him what he was doing and he told her he was technically still attached to the stairs. Granny almost fell over with laughter as well as the rest of the house. I remember feeling sad thinking I wish I had been born to Granny Milly instead of my cruel mother.

We lived in an old half of a company house that was built back in the wartime for soldiers and their families. The only source of heat was the coal stove in the kitchen and a fireplace in the living room. The walls were lath and plaster. Insulation was made of old newspapers stuffed in the cracks on the walls. Winter days on those stairs were so cold that every bone in my body ached. When the long days of sitting on the stairs were finally over it was no better going to bed in those unheated bedrooms, laying under the one thin blanket we had been given. We had to put on extra layers of clothes just to be warm enough to go to sleep. How I hated those nights curling up into a small ball on my bottom bunk with my nose so cold watching Ann's breath as she whispered to me from the top bunk.

Ann was my confidante sometimes, because we shared a small room and got along pretty well most of the time. I do remember one time though when my temper reached a boiling point with Ann and I had stolen the electric tape from the tool chest and made a line cutting the room in half. she was no longer allowed to step on my side of the room making it very difficult for her to go to bed that night because the set of bunk beds we shared were on my side of the bedroom, out of fear of what I would do to her and what may have happened had she told mother she sat in the corner for what seemed hours crying until my guilt got the best of me and I pulled the tape up to let her cross thus giving my two brothers Vin and Joe the same idea. They slept on the bunk beds in the room next to ours. I would often lie there on my top bunk on those cold nights and wonder if they felt as cold and alone as I did.

Mother and George got the biggest room and the only one with a vent cut in the floor so the heat would rise from the stove in the kitchen, sending some warmth up making their room almost bearable to sleep in.

Mother would see the hunger in our eyes, and get us in the middle of the kitchen floor to fight it out. Whoever won got the crust. Funny, I was the smallest, but I was the strongest. 9 times out of 10 I would win the fight. The dry taste of crust crumbling in my mouth combined with the guilt over beating up my sister and brothers didn't seem worth it, but the hunger won.

Back to the story.

Lies and more Lies

George told my mother that one of us had drank his precious Pepsi. Naturally, all of us denied it. My mother questioned us one by one, and came to the conclusion (as she usually did) that I was the one who was lying. I swore it wasn't me, and it really wasn't.

So my mother, who had me convinced that even if I swore on a stack of bibles, I still wouldn't know what the truth was, immediately proceeded to beat me. She beat me with everything she could get her hands on, and every ounce of energy she had. That was how the cut came to be on my eye.

In her rage, and fury, she pulled the nearly empty milk jug out of the fridge, and proceeded to beat me multiple times over my head with it. I saw blood spurting out, realized it was mine, and panicked, thinking she was going to kill me. As a survival mechanism, I decided to confess that it was indeed me who had consumed the Pepsi, and that I was sorry. In my mind, to this day I still hear the screams from that day. The screams of that little girl I once was.

I guess that's when she really lost it. I think I started to black out. She was beating me with the coal shovel when George came into the kitchen.

George: *"Stop! You're going to kill her!!"*

She stopped, looking at me with such anger and hatred, that it still haunts me to this day.

All was quiet for about 10 minutes until Vin came in and whispered something in my mother's ear. Before I could protect myself from what was coming, the leather belt slammed across my back, with such force I couldn't breathe for what seemed like a whole minute. Apparently my brother had drank the precious Pepsi, and decided now to admit to it, now that I was half

16

dead or at least felt like I was. So then I got an even worse beating for lying. I missed a whole week of school because I wasn't able to even hold a pen or pencil in my hand.

What happened to Vin you ask- absolutely nothing? He could never do anything wrong in my mother's eyes.

So I told my Granny Milly the whole awful story. I'm sure she had no idea how ashamed I felt for letting out our family's dirty little (BIG) secrets. She just rubbed my head while I cried, and told me everything was going to be alright. I remember thinking all the while about the beating I was going to get, but not really caring because in that moment, I was being loved.

About a half hour later, I heard the old red car coming down the road getting ready to turn up the lane. Fear gripped my heart so tightly that I thought for sure I was going to die on the spot. I begged my Granny not to say anything, promising to clean her toilet with a toothbrush, or pick as many blueberries as she needed for pie sales. She gently took my hand, and told Minny to take me down to hide behind the bushes by Walter's Lane.

Walter was Granny Millie's neighbor and he literally lived at the end of a lane on the edge of Granny's property. He came over every day to eat as he was a lonely old man. Granny once told me in passing that his house was just as run down as grannies. He had a family at one point but his only child, a boy named john was taken into the spirit world suddenly. The boy was bullied so much at school that Walter came home one day to find the boy had hung himself in the closet. After that, his wife left unable to deal with the loss of their only child. Poor Walter never recovered emotionally and let his house fall apart. Unable to cook or care for himself he left his job of over 20 years and granny even had to sometimes tell him to go home and take a bath he smelled so bad as there were no showers back then. I always just seemed to sense sadness with him I couldn't quite explain.

17

I just stood there holding my breath for what seemed like an eternity. But when I think back on it now, that entire day, it seemed to take an eternity to get home. It was like the faster we ran; the greater the fear seemed to well up inside of me. The fear of what mother was going to do once she got a hold of me. It almost seemed to pull me back up the lane to Granny Millie's, but we finally reached the hiding spot at the end of the lane.

I could hear mother and Granny Milly yelling at each other like they were right next to me. My mother was calling to me as I hid with Minny. I knew the consequences, but I wasn't ready - or willing - to face them, so we remained hidden long after she was gone. In fact, we stayed there until it was almost too dark to find our way home. Finally, I found my legs, and we made our way back. I was so afraid that mother was parked at the end of the lane waiting for me; I almost didn't bother going back.

When we got to the house, it was as though nothing had happened. Cat gave me her "jammies" to wear, and we all sat down to have hot blueberry pie.

I think I was there for a couple of days before my mother came to get me. Not a word was said. I didn't even get the beating I had been expecting. I didn't, however, see my Granny for a long time after that. I think maybe I expected great changes that day, but nothing changed except the anger inside me that grew, and festered like an open wound that would never heal.

***

CHAPTER 2

Superstitious

I found the ace of spades today – the card of death - underneath my bed. My heart instantly went to my throat because the ace of spades is a sign of death (at least that's what the adults made us kids believe). From my recollection it had something to do with the soldiers back in past wartimes, when it was common practice to leave a card, the ace of spades, on the bodies of the dead soldiers.

<u>Living In Fear of Superstitions</u>

The small town where I am come from had so many superstitions. In such an isolated community it was inevitable that superstitions lived long lives. Some were silly, yet some were so believable they would make the hair stand up on the back of your neck. Whether they were silly or not though didn't matter as we still lived by them and continue to do so to this day.

One of the silliest ones I had heard over the years was that if you drop an umbrella on the floor there will be a murder in the house. Another silly one I had heard was that after you see an ambulance you must hold your breath until you saw a black or brown dog. There were the more serious ones we lived by - and I still do to this day - like its bad luck to enter through one door and leave through a different door. Then there's the one that proved true many times over the years - a spoon to the floor, a stranger to the door. If you see a black cat I have to make the sign of 3 X's with your finger on your left hand and whoever is with you has to do the same. It's just the way things have been for so long it's like second nature.

My great "Grandma" Linster, that was Granny Millie's mother, was a tealeaf reader. She was very good at it too, from what I heard when I was listening to conversations I wasn't supposed to hear.

She was always giving us warnings.

"Be careful," she would warn, if a bird flew to close to the house.

"If that damn bird gets in here, someone will die."

If the bird flew close enough to the window and actually hit it, she would run outside to check to see if it was still alive. She would then tell us that if it were only slightly stunned, there would be a sickness in the family. But if the bird actually broke its neck a child would be 'passing to the other side' as she liked to call it.

Funny, I seem to remember a lot of birds trying to fly through our windows when I was a child. Each time, one of the adults would run out to check to see if the damn bird was still breathing. All of us children would stand there waiting and watching to see if one of us was going to 'pass to the other side'. Finally, after what seemed like an eternity, the adult, whichever one of them had went to check, would come into the house with either the good or bad news.

Anyways, back to the ace of spades. My Grandma Linster didn't read cards very often, she would read just a plain ole' deck of playing cards but every card in the deck had some kind of meaning behind them, and she was oh so very good at reading those cards. People on Cape Breton Island though thought it was the work of the devil.

Funny though, they didn't think there was anything wrong with the tealeaf readings she did on a daily basis. I saw her do her card reading a couple of times. She read just plain old playing cards not like all the different kinds of tarot cards they use today. I would watch in total awe as people would take up her every word, barely breathing and never speaking for fear they might miss something she said. At the time, I didn't really know what the ace of spades meant, but whenever I saw my Grandma pull it out of the deck as the first card; she would start to mutter as if she was under a spell herself, what seemed like some kind of a spell in a language I couldn't quite understand.

Mothers Demands

While I could hear my mother yelling at me from the kitchen to get the coal in for the night's fire, even though it was only 3 in the afternoon, I stood there paralyzed with fear, unable to move or speak because of the cursed ace of spades I had found in my room. I didn't want to pick up that awful card. But if I didn't, and someone else found it, what would happen to me? I was already considered to be evil by my mother, and stepfather, so, if anyone found it, mother would surely beat me to death for having it. I couldn't understand where this card had come from. We didn't own a deck of cards because they were considered the "devil's hands".

By this time, my mother was now heading up the stairs. I could hear the belt cracking off the wall. I quickly hid the card under a piece of carpet in the corner of my closet. Before I was even standing up again, down came the belt and all of her fury with it.

"You stupid little tramp!" she screamed,

"When I call to you, you better get your fat ass down those stairs, or next time I will kill you, so help me God!"

Then, she proceeded to beat me in the usual fashion, grabbing my hair as tightly as she could, while beating me with all of the strength left in her body. She screamed the same things over and over again in my ear as she always did.

"You stupid little tramp, I never wanted you,"

"You're evil,"

"The devil is gonna come and get you in the middle of the night, and take you back to hell

where you belong."

I think that after a while, I had become used to the beatings, or maybe it was that I just didn't care anymore.

But still I screamed the same things I always did. *"I'm sorry mommy," "I swear I will be a good girl," "I will listen, I swear."*

For some sick, unknown reason that still baffles me; she would stop, smile and just leave. As she was leaving, she screamed *"You better get that coal in, if you know what's good for you. You little tramp."*

I quickly pushed the ace of spades further under the carpet, just to be sure that no one would find it. I wiped the blood off my lip, and went to the barn to get the coal for the night.

Who could I talk to about that dreadful ace of spades? Was I really a product of the devil? Did he put it there under my bed to show me that he owned my soul?

Marlie's Advice

Like a bolt of lightning hitting me in the head, I thought of Marley. She was a woman I babysat for once in a while, when I was allowed out, or when my mother needed to go to town or to buy us clothes for school, and needed the extra money. Marley didn't believe in all of the hocus-pocus of our little town. She was shunned by most of the people that lived there, but she really didn't care. Her husband was an alcoholic who fixed the townspeople's cars. I think that about the only time people were ever nice to her, or him, was when they wanted something.

I have a lot of good memories from my childhood. Unfortunately, none with my own mother or stepfather. Most were with Marley and Johnny. They would buy me a special treat whenever they went out. Sometimes Johnny would slip me a drink of rum, when Marley was waiting in the car. I would gulp it down like a parched man in the desert dying of thirst. Then, I'd brush my teeth about 50 times before it was time to go home, terrified that someone would catch a smell of liquor on my breath.

I remember being younger back when my parents were still married and my father gave us a bottle of beer with a little bit left in it, this was called the toe nail because it was apparently the worse part of the beer and oh how I hated the taste. That was the way it was in our town, parents gave their kids beer to sip on no harm in it. Even when babies were teething they got a shot of liquor in their bottle to go to bed and a little rubbed on their gums to ease the pain.

My brother Joe I remember one time we had found a half full bottle on the porch and drank it down thinking he was drinking beer but it was actually oil he had drank. They both tasted the same to him maybe, it was just a bitter gross taste, it almost killed him, and he had to go to the hospital to get his stomach pumped. When I took a drink at Johnny's it was that feeling I liked, that warm sensation as the booze that settled into the pit of my stomach that I liked so much and would grow to love as years passed by.

Marley even owned a deck of cards, with which she taught me how to play rummy. I was so obsessed with the game whenever I would be called on to baby-sit for Marley, she would get me to come an hour or so early to play a quick game of rummy. I would go home and dream about it every night.

Boy, if my mother knew about those dreams, she would have killed me. I had to find a way to talk to Marley. I just wasn't sure how to do it without getting caught. As luck would have it, after I dragged in 3 five gallon buckets of coal and fed the chickens, my mother asked me to go to the store to get her tobacco. It was at least a half hour walk there, and another half hour back, but I knew if I ran once I was out of sight I could slip through the back yards, and no one would be the wiser.

I ran as fast as I could. On the final leg of my journey, I had to climb old Freddy's fence. I was sure I wasn't going to make it, but I knew I had to do it, as my life, or should I say my soul, depended on it. Huffing and puffing and shaking from the adrenalin rush I was feeling , I didn't even bother knocking, which was considered pretty rude in those days, but I had no time to think about that. I had to get to Marley.

"Help me Marley!" I said in between gasps of air. Quickly I told her about the dreaded ace of spades, and then I just burst into tears. There was something about knowing you were going to hell that was very frightening. *"Hush child!"* she said. She might not have believed in any of that stuff, but she certainly knew what to do in situations like this one.

"First," she said to me, *"You don't belong to the devil and you are definitely not going to hell. I see the way you look after those animals. Someone who cares the way you do doesn't belong to the devil."*

"Second, you must go home and burn the card by the moonlight, and be careful that you aren't caught. Say this chant three times and you should be fine." I so wanted to ask her where the card might have come from but I knew there was no time. I was sure my mother was watching the clock s we spoke. I quickly left the house, climbed old Freddy's fence, and ran all

the way to the store. When I got there, Gerald the store owner offered me a ride home. I gladly took it in hopes to avoid mother's wrath for being late.

I got home just in the nick of time. My mother was sitting at the table having tea with one of the neighbors. Good, I was safe.
"Time for bed" she said, even though it was only 8 o'clock at night. But I wouldn't dare
argue with her. I just did as I was told. I went upstairs, and as I climbed into the top bunk, a feeling of utter sadness came over me. I wept, and worried

about someone finding that card. I tried my hardest to stay awake, but I cried myself to sleep.

Sometime in the middle of the night I rolled over, and there was old Frankie, standing over my bed with a big butcher knife in his hand. He was also an outcast in our town, and was considered to be evil. He lived with his blind brother in a little run down shack on the outskirts of town. I let out a blood curdling scream out of me.

You see, in our town no one had locks on their doors. There were no police and no crimes... well, except for all of the child molesters, wife beaters and child abusers. But no one ever talked about them. Everyone just turned a blind eye. Like I said before everything was kept a secret in our little town.

My mother and stepfather came running. When they flicked on the light, the shadow of Frankie was gone. I was so hysterical that I could barely tell them what was going on. When I finally did, George checked under my bed and in the closet. He checked the whole house but couldn't find anything. When he was finally done, my mother said, *"You see, I told you she belonged to the devil."*

I had to burn that card. I waited until everyone was asleep. I hung out the window and recited the chant that Marley had given me. Then I went to bed and prayed. I prayed most of the night, until I could see the first signs of daylight, praying for God to take my soul to heaven if I was to die. I just wasn't sure if he was listening.

***

Chapter 3

Mother

Anger, hate, rage, confusion…all summarize what I felt and thought every time I thought of mother. Fear; let's not forget the constant fear. Terror was something she had instilled in all of us kids. From the time we were born into this world, it was something I also think that we all carry with us even to this day. It was never kindness, love or affection or any of the things normal people think about when they think of the woman who gave birth to them.

I sometimes sit very still and try to recall some happy memory from my past but I usually fail miserably and end up crying in frustration of tears and anger. There was nothing happy about living in fear every single day of my life. I suppose I could ever-so-sarcastically talk about going to pick blueberries in the heat of the blazing August sun. It wasn't a pleasure most of the time, but a chore. Mother would grab the container full of blueberries from our small hands and start picking through them pouring them into another plastic bowl searching for leaves from our sloppy picking. The more leaves we picked the more she had to touch the berries. Touching them too much before they were sold was an unforgivable sin in mother's eyes because they would become bruised and black, no longer the brilliant blue shine on them that made them so appealing to buy.

Mother did have a trick to fool people though, she would always put aside two cups of the best berries to put on top of the container so most people wouldn't know they were badly bruised. This trick however didn't stop her from lashing out her fury on us kids for our incompetence and carelessness for not paying enough attention to what we were doing. After so many leaves were found she would start to count and then the fear would set in because I knew what was going to happen for every leaf she would find; it would be one whack with the belt. Interestingly, to this day I can't stand the sight of a blueberry.

Mother came from a big family, as most of the families were large in the small towns that lined the coast of Cape Breton Island. She was the oldest of 15 siblings. There was a child born before her, and her name was Lucy Diane, but she died just a few days after her birth. No one ever really explained why. Granny Milly would just say that no parent should ever outlive their children. It took her many years to get over the death of her firstborn.

I'm really not sure what life was like for mother growing up. She would sometimes tell stories about how hard it was growing up working as a strip miner from a very young age.

A strip mine was a very deep hole dug into the ground. It was so deep you had to be lowered in an old washbasin down into the cold, dark ground picking the coal along the way and putting it into the washtub. Once the tub was full you would tug the rope to be pulled back to the surface.

The town made it illegal to strip mine after a while because folks would leave open shafts all over the place, without a warning sign. Some people who fell in the hole were never found again. Mother was claustrophobic and I can't help but wonder if this had anything to do with it. I remember one time the bathroom door got stuck and she couldn't get out. She was going crazy and George had to put the ladder up to the bathroom window to get her out I had never seen her in such a state I wanted to laugh and cry at the same time listening to her screams from the other side of the door. My sister Ann was about to just completely give up. I remember her saying to me *"Boy she was a good cook though wasn't she?"* Mother didn't think this was so funny and Ann got a good beating for her words.

Mother's family was always divided in some way, fighting over God only knows what. Seven family members on one side not speaking to the other 7 family members on the other side and one always stuck in the middle as the go between. There always seemed to be some kind of family feud going on. I say 7 on each side because mother had a brother Gerry, who was the oldest but not considered a member of the family (by half of the family).

He went to prison for murder after he killed his wife in a fit of jealous rage leaving behind 2 babies. No one in the family wanted to take in the babies with folks in our small town whispering about how their father had killed their mother as they walked on by. At least that was how Granny Milly explained it to me.

Mother herself was divided most of the time. When someone would come to visit, mother had her best fake smile mask on as she sat there and gossiped for hours to whoever she was sitting with. They would talk about anybody and everybody.

It didn't matter what they talked about. She would sit and talk to her friends for what seemed like forever. Everyone in the whole town knew all of your business and you didn't even have to ever leave the house. In those days we had party lines on the phones so you would listen in to other people's conversations and then carry the gossip to the neighbors' house. Once they had left, she would turn to George my stepfather and complain about whoever it was that was visiting her for the afternoon.

That's what mother did, she complained about everything but when she wasn't complaining she was yelling or smacking one of us kids, so I would rather hear her complaining to George. People said my mother was beautiful just like Marilyn Monroe with her blond curly hair with beautiful white teeth. Funny, when I looked at her I didn't see any of this; she looked like a monster no matter how nice her hair or clothes were!

Then there was the odd day when she was in a good mood and Ann and I would be allowed into her bedroom to sit on her bed and watch her get ready to go shopping. She would carefully apply her mascara and a bit of lipstick, topped off with face cream.

I would love looking on her dresser at all her fancy jewelry, even though I doubted any of it was real. I would never have touched it, as God only knows how she would have reacted!

My stepfather George had married my mother shortly after she left my real father. Rumor had it that they were messing around for quite some time before she left my father, even though George was a man of the cloth. I don't think it was long after they were married before we moved to the small town of Donkin.

Small Town Gossip

There was nothing in Donkin since it was such a small place. The only business in town was a store called the Co-Op that carried your basic necessities and groceries. Everyone in the town had a charge account there. The building still stands today, just an old empty shell of what it used to be. It's all boarded up standing all alone at the bottom of the big hill that leads you to our little town.

There were only other 2 buildings, and really I wouldn't call them buildings, both were only 2 stories high. The post office was made of brick and the legion was made of aluminum siding but both were in need of some serious repair. I swear everyone in the town except mother and George went to the legion on Friday and Saturday nights. Neither one of them drank; although I had often wished they did just from watching the happy people coming and going from the legion.

Everyone would gather at the post office on Monday mornings after a wild weekend at the legion and the talk would start. Who had made a fool of themselves, who left with whom, who was fighting and so on and so forth. Mother had no complaints about going to pick up the mail on Mondays; she certainly didn't want to miss out on the gossip for the week. Yes indeed, small town gossip was very much alive in our small town on Monday mornings.

George was a short man with very dark skin. He always wore a stocking hat, even on the hottest day of the year. He worked at the local ice rink - or the old forum as everyone called it. The old forum was in the next town over from ours so us kids never really got a chance to go there I can remember maybe 4 or 5 times in my childhood going there and I'm not sure if any of them were trips with mother and George. Perhaps they were school trips.

He was never mean to any of us kids. All he ever seemed to do was read all of these religious books, and watch church shows on television like Earnest Ainslie. He was a television evangelist on every Sunday night preaching about sin and how it ruined lives and families. Oh how I hated the sound of that voice booming from the television every week. I think the only conversations George ever had with us were about God and how if we did something wrong we would surely be punished.

Fear of God is what he instilled in all of us kids from the many years of listening to his preaching. That was my biggest worry as a child - being punished by God or the devil stealing my soul. I still worry about it sometimes even to this day. He would preach the 10 commandments to us on a daily basis drilling them into our heads and telling us what they meant and how we were breaking the laws of God. Terrified would not begin to describe how I felt about breaking these laws:

1. Thou shalt have no other gods before me.

2. Thou shalt not make unto thee any graven image,

3. Thou shalt not take the name of the Lord thy God in vain;

4. Remember the Sabbath day, to keep it holy.

5. Honor thy father and thy mother:

6. Thou shalt not kill.

7. Thou shalt not commit adultery.

8. Thou shalt not steal.

9. Thou shalt not bear false witness against thy neighbor.

10. Thou shalt not covet thy neighbor's house

Each one of these commandments had a special meaning and a special punishment if we were to break them.

There was the odd time he would interfere with mother's beatings or punishments, then she would turn and lash out at him screaming obscenities and smashing him with whatever she could grab. I remember one day she picked up a log and started beating him over the back of the head with it. He reacted like he was one of us kids at first covering his head and trying to cower by the stairs. Then he turned around grabbed the log, threw it on the floor and started yelling at her.

That was the one and only time I ever heard George yell or raise his voice. He was drunk after that for about a week. That's when I found out that George had a drinking problem and that's why neither one of them ever went to the legion on a Friday or Saturday night. George was apparently an alcoholic. Once he got started with that first drink nothing would stop him from getting more. Funny thing is, years later I would suffer from the same affliction.

The whole town was talking about it, for what seemed like forever, about how mother had driven him back to the bottle. Mother threatened to leave him after a week and life went on as usual.

***

CHAPTER 4

Run, Run Away

I woke the next morning to a cup of ice-cold water being thrown in my face. This wasn't unusual however, this was the way I woke up every day for as long as I could remember living at home with mother.

The same scenario played out the same way every single day for years. I could hear Mother stomping up the stairs, turning on the tap in the bathroom filling up the big plastic yellow cup with icy cold tap water. Yet try as I might I could never seem to open my eyes and sit up before she burst through the door. By this point it was too late. The ice cold water would hit my face and brutally shock my system awake. The tears of self-pity and anger at my own stupidity for not waking up would then start to flow. Mother really seemed to take great pleasure in my misery and pain.

Day Dreams

As a kid, I always loved country music. That was all anyone ever listened to in our town. Rock music like Metallica or Led Zeppelin was never allowed. It was considered the devil's music. The soothing sound of the guitar playing on the old radio seemed to take me away from wherever I was at that time usually that was in the back yard on the old wooden swing .

When I was grounded, I used to sit for hours on the homemade swing outside, singing to myself, and dreaming of the day when I would leave this Godforsaken place, and become a big famous singer. That never happened, but dream did and it was what I needed to keep me sane.

It seems to me when I think back, I was always grounded. Even in the winter, I would sit outside on that old swing. Not that I even liked it, but it was better than being inside, waiting to get a beating for something I did (or didn't do).

One day I was sitting there, grounded and day dreaming as usual when an idea came to me that wouldn't go away. I could just run away. Run away, live in the woods until I was old enough to get a job, and never have to look at my awful mother or stepfather again.

Sitting there smiling, I felt almost guilty with pleasure. No more beatings, no more aching arms from using that heavy bucksaw to cut the wood to warm the house.

Everyone worked hard in my family, either cutting and splitting wood or picking coal from the shore to try to keep the house warm for winter. We would start at the end of May and continue right up to the end of September before it got to cold.

Undertow

Every day after school, George would put the old rusty buck saw and some brim bags for the coal in the trunk of the old red car and off we would all go down the old shore road to begin our long day of work. We would walk along the shore for miles one way then turn around and walk miles back picking up little pieces of coal that lay among the rocks. We filled the brim bags with as much as our little arms could carry. Mother never came with us though and with good reason since her and her friend Valery used to go for walks along the shore. One day they came across something that looked like an old garbage bag but once they got close enough they realized it was a man's body. He had got caught up in the undertow a few towns over and drowned. An undertow was a current that ran not too far from the shore pulling bodies out to sea stealing souls to feed the ocean .The search and rescue were still looking for him when they found the body. I'm not sure if either one of them ever went back to the shore after that day.

Once school was out for the summer, there was gardening to do, chickens to be fed and so on. We raised chickens, turkeys, pigeons and geese for winter food and also to sell for extra money for things like shoes and clothes. There never seemed to be enough time to do all the chores though.

Just thinking about running away, I was almost giddy. No more going to the shore, walking 10 miles each way for a lousy bagful of coal. Only to come home to hear from mother that it wasn't enough and we were all going to freeze this winter if we didn't get our lazy arses in gear. Just think, just think....

I'm a bit obsessive, which I certainly didn't realize at the time. I thought and thought about my plan to be free for what seemed like weeks. It might not have been that long, but it sure seemed like it.

Every time my mother looked at me, I was sure she knew what I was thinking, and the knot of fear in my stomach just grew bigger and bigger. I had the opportunity to run away several times, but I was just too chicken to take it.

One time, my mother went to the women's lodge for a penny sale. I was supposed to go with her, but I forced myself to throw up on the kitchen floor, just because I knew this was going to be my opportunity to leave and run away from the rotten life I had been born and trapped into. I got my face scrubbed in the vomit, and a beating I would like to forget, but I did it all just for that chance. I was so peeved at myself for not taking it, but fear prevented me, and I didn't go.

There was one other time I ran away, which even today is still vivid in my mind. It was when my mother and father were still married. They were sleeping. I don't remember how old I was but I was very young. I remember packing my clothes in a paper bag, and sneaking out the door, crying my eyes out. I don't know why I was crying, I just know I was very sad. I snuck out the door and went to the old bus garage. It was raining out cold and damp. I remember that even at such a young age closing that door behind me, I felt free.

I am not sure how long I was there, but a bus driver walked up to me, asked me some questions, and then took me back to my house. I remember clearly when he left. My mother told me if I wanted to leave, I should, because she didn't want me anyway. She proceeded to pack my clothes into a paper grocery bag, and sent me on my way. I left happy, because she was giving me my freedom, but once I got to the end of the driveway I started to cry. When my aunt Marie came out to get me, I was crying so hard that I didn't even understand why. At least I felt like my aunt Marie understood why I was in such a state. Now I know it was because I didn't have my mother's love or understanding.

So I waited for my chance. Then one day my mother asked me to go pick blueberries to make some money to help out with buying a bun of bread and milk for her and George's morning tea. Back then, you got a dollar for a quart of berries, which was a lot of money.

Blueberry picking was a great pastime when you grew up in a small town like mine where there was really nothing else to do during those long August days to pass the time. If you were actually picking blueberries for yourself, instead of money for something for the house, it made it so worth it to work under the scorching sun.

The only trick was not to eat even one. If you ate that one, you would look as though you never got any picked, because you would spend the whole day eating. Funny, I couldn't even lie. All Mother had to do was to tell me to stick out my tongue, and it would be blue. Boy, oh boy, would I be in trouble!

So I grabbed the plastic yellow 4 quart bowl and a cup. It always seemed easier to fill the cup than the bowl. It never seemed to take as long as I expected.

I didn't think I would have the opportunity to run, because usually my sister Ann followed wherever I went. As far as my mother was concerned I couldn't be trusted. I was told I would be caught doing bad, bad things with boys. Now I know it was sex, but at the time I really had no idea what my mother was talking about.

When I found out Ann wasn't coming, I really wasn't sure if I was relieved, or scared, because I knew what was on my mind. Freedom, freedom from being a product of the devil, freedom from the beating, just basically freedom from everything.

I didn't know what freedom felt like, but I knew it was going to feel good. Normally I would head out to Andrew's field to pick the blueberries, but this time I walked across the field, got behind a tree, and crawled all the way to the end of the road in a mud-caked ditch. There was nothing stopping me now.

I figured the only place no one would dare look for me was in the woods behind old Frankie's house, so I headed there as fast as my little stubby legs could carry me. The house loomed before me like something from "Friday the 13th" At least I thought it did, since that was the only scary movie I had ever seen.

It was really just an old, run down shack, but, it scared the hell out of me knowing I was going to have to cross his yard to get to the woods. I sat and waited in the ditch to see if Frankie had gone to the legion, or just his blind brother Peano was home. I'd forgotten that they had a German Shepherd. He began to bark wildly as if he was sensing my presence. Thank God they kept him on a short leash!

Waiting for my heart to return from my throat to my chest, I just sat and listened. I'm not sure how long I listened, but I know it was quite a long time, long enough to know that Frankie wasn't there, because if he was, I would have heard him yelling at the stupid dog to shut up. It seemed whenever he was around, the dog would just go nuts. Everyone said it was because the dog could see the devil in him.

So once I was sure he wasn't home, I made a mad dash for the woods. I could hear Peano yelling, and the dog going crazy, but I ran anyway, ran until I thought and felt my heart would burst. Once I got into the trees, I realized I wasn't as prepared as I thought I was, nor was I as smart. The first couple of hours were great, but then I got hungry, and sick of eating blueberries.

I think I realized then that I needed a better plan. By this time, I had been gone far too long, and I was scared to go out to the road. It was getting dark in the woods, so I accepted the fact that I was defeated.

So, with a great effort, I picked myself up, and headed for the road, knowing what was awaiting me when I got home. I didn't have to wait very long.

I guess my mother was driving around the big loop we call our town, and caught me walking back without a single blueberry in my yellow bowl. She didn't even wait for me to get close to the car. She jumped out, fists flying as usual. I didn't even have time to tell her the lie I had thought about all day.

I don't remember much after that, just waking up so sore I couldn't move. I was grounded for so long after that I had pretty much lost all hope of ever fulfilling my dream of being free. Then one day, something wonderful happened.

We raised a lot of animals, not as pets, but for food because we were so poor. One day, some of the pigeons, yes, we ate pigeons, got caught up in the mesh wire in their little cage behind the barn. No matter how hard everyone else tried, they couldn't fit into that small little hole to get the pigeons. Eventually they decided to trust me to go outside and try. With all eyes watching me, I carefully climbed into that small little hole filled with all kinds of pigeon droppings, and grabbed them one by one to bring them to safety, only to find out later that the reason for the great need was because they were supper.

Once I had finished climbing out of the hole, I felt completely victorious. My mother and stepfather then informed me, that they thought I was no longer a bad girl, and was allowed out into the back yard whenever I wanted. It wasn't the best deal I got, but at least I was allowed out. Now I could sit on that old wooden swing and dream of my freedom once again.

***

CHAPTER 5

Ann

My mother, in all of her fury and anger, could never seem to give my sister Ann and I, any kind of love. I often wondered after having a few kids of my own how she could be just oh- so-cold and completely unloving all the time. Eventually though there comes a time when you have to stop thinking about it and just accept that that's just the way it (and she) was.

Ann's Name's Origins

My sister Ann was the youngest of us all. Joe and I were just nine months apart. I don't think my mother had ever heard of birth control, and Vin and I were almost 11 months apart. Ann was born almost 2 years after Joe. Mother said she named her after a nurse in the hospital. She said, by this point she didn't want any more kids, so she didn't even bother picking out a name for poor Ann. Talk about feeling unwanted.

My poor sister almost got it as bad as me some days. Beatings with the broom seemed to be mother's personalized torturous way of punishing her. Ann would always make this face without even realizing she was doing it. I can't really describe it, it was kind of like a half smile and mother hated it. Whenever Ann made this face, mother would yell and scream, calling her 'grinny' and lunge at her with the broom or whatever she had in her hand at the moment. If nothing was close she would pound on Ann with her fists of fury. The same thing she seemed to do with me on a daily basis.

I remember all of us teasing Ann relentlessly at mother's beckoning, singing a song that was playing on the radio. It was called Nelly and went something like this,

"The day that Nelly died she set me by her side and gave me a pair of smelly drawers they were baggy at the knees and full of flies and fleas but those

were the drawers that Nelly wore. She was 6 feet underground but the smell was still around cause those were the drawers that Nelly wore."

Over and over we would tease Ann by singing this song. Never once did it occur to us that we were hurting her feelings back then. It really was survival of the fittest. That's probably why Ann was constantly rooting around in the room we shared together to try to find things to get me into trouble and score brownie points for herself (and probably to get back at me for the hurtful words I would say to her day in and day out).

Sometimes I used to think Ann was so much like one of the nosey neighbors that lived on our street. She was always waiting to find something in our room that I had stashed so she could have something to talk to her friends about.

A Woman's Curse

I remember when I started my period, I was nine at the time. In my mind, way too early to begin my trip into womanhood. We were taught (loose term) sex education class in school that year, I believe it was grade 5. This was the year of changes and the beginning of my real rebellion. I had to bring home a permission slip for mother to sign before I could take the sex education class I was so awkward and embarrassed and mother wasn't exactly too happy about it either.

She ranted and raved to anyone who would listen about how it wasn't right that we were taught that filth in our school systems. She said that she never had to take anything like that when she was in school which in my opinion is why she had popped out 4 kids before the age of 20. I sat through the whole class, my face flaming red, not really absorbing too much because of my own self-consciousness. I just felt so uncomfortable with the whole "becoming a woman thing". Mother didn't help my situation much; she was never approachable in any situation, never mind helping with all of

40

the things that are supposed to happen naturally to young girls as they grow. These things were just completely unacceptable as far as mother was concerned.

When I finally started my period, mother took some maxi-pads out of the grocery bag, handed them to me and ordered me to go put them in the top of the closet in my room. I remember feeling so much shame as I tucked them under my arm, hurrying up the stairs before anyone would see me. I would feel that shame and embarrassment every single time I would start my period and have to go and ask mother for maxi pads.

So I took them and hid them in the top of our closet to be used when I got the curse - as it was called back in those days. Once you had it that meant you could pop out a baby at any time. At least that's what all of us kids thought. We didn't realize there was a whole act you had to perform to get to the stage of pregnancy. Myths and rumors are what we lived by and thrived on.

It was like a huge shame growing into a woman according to mother. Once, Ann found them and, not having a clue what they were, she proudly marched down the stairs waving one in the air in front of mother and her visiting company to ask why there were giant band aids in the top of the closet! I was completely and utterly mortified. I wanted to crawl away and never be seen again. Mother laughed it off with her company there but I knew the moment they were gone I was going to be in so much trouble.

I often wondered why Ann did this type of thing. I would get so angry at her maybe she really didn't know any different, but if she did I can only imagine it was for the same reasons I did stupid things like that - to get mother's mind off of me and onto her.

The punishment for Ann finding the maxi pads wasn't as bad as I imagined it would be. I was just grounded as usual to my room. I went, grateful I didn't get a good beating.

That was the day when we had one of the worse storms I can remember as a child, the cold wind and snow raging outside pelting against my bedroom window, the snow just seemed to get deeper and deeper with each passing moment. I was so bored and so cold my fingertips were actually numb I had to keep breathing on them to stop the sting. No heat got into my bedroom with the door closed and I wasn't allowed to keep the door opened when I was grounded, no matter how cold it got in my bedroom. I only had this one thin blanket to wrap around my body to try to warm up, but it was not doing any good against the cold January winds. In total frustration, silent tears slid down my cheeks and then got cold as they dried. There was nothing to do but sit on the edge of my bunk bed and think.

Young Inventor

I started playing around on a small electric piano I had bought at a penny sale for a dime. At the time, I wasn't sure why I wanted to buy the piano other than it would be a good way to pass time when I was grounded (and I had a lot of grounded time!). It never had any batteries in it, and being as poor as we were, I doubted it would ever see batteries.

I stared at that little piano until it was time for supper, thinking the whole time about a way I could get this mini-piano working.

Thinking seemed to be the one thing that got me into trouble all the time. Grounded or not, we still ate together every night, just like a perfect little family. Afterwards, Ann and I would always have to wash the dishes. I knew I was going to be grounded for a while, and I just couldn't stand the thought of sitting up in a freezing cold room tonight, or any other night for that matter. I decided to steal a butter knife from the kitchen to wire the little piano with an old lamp cord I had hidden in the top of my closet (for what purpose I was not really sure).

In my mind it made perfect sense. One of the many great plans I would hatch over the years. I would wire it up, turn it on low, and teach myself how to play the piano. I had great dreams of becoming someone famous, maybe even a world-renowned piano player.

My grandfather was a jack-of-all-trades, master of none as the old saying goes. He taught us things he thought were important in life, like fixing car engines or rewiring electrical outlets. He always said we would use it no matter where we were at in our life. And he was right, I was about to use one of the skills he had taught me.

Once supper was over and the dishes had to be done immediately (with mother there was no waiting), Ann would go to the bathroom, just like she always did whenever the dishes had to be done. It would slow us down so much; my mother would come out with a broom, and start bashing me over the head in a rage as she was most of the time. I was always the one who had to wash, therefore, I was the one being too slow, and messing around. Never did it occur to me that the sink full of dishes I could start drying to catch up , I swear, Ann did it just to get me in trouble!

Tonight though, I really didn't care. All I could think about was where I was going to put that butter knife so I could get safely to my room without getting caught. As soon as Ann was out of sight, I took it, and stuffed it in my sock as quickly as I could, hoping it wouldn't fall out the bottom (I had holes in my sock). I don't recall any of us kids owning a decent pair of socks and I can really never remember getting new ones for that matter.

When Ann returned, I continued washing the dishes as usual, as if nothing had happened. I went upstairs and shut the door tightly behind me. I sat and listened for about 40 minutes before I had the guts to do anything. Climbing to the top of the closet, I grabbed the old plug and proceeded to strip the wire. It was a lot more difficult than I had imagined. It took me what seemed like forever, but I finally got the wires stripped. This was something I had learned from watching my grandfather. However, when I had watched him do it, it seemed to be effortless for him. For me it was a mighty struggle.

Buck Jack of All Trades

My grandfather's name was Buck. Even his own kids called him Buck, I never really found out why. He was hurt while working at the Number 26 Colliery that was the mine most of my family had worked in since they were just small children. My father was pulled out of school in grade 3 to go work in the coal mine and support his family.

That's just the way it was back then. My uncle Jackie had died in the explosion at the Number 26 colliery. My father had just finished his shift and came up from the underground when the mine exploded. I think my grandfather was hurt many years before I was born in a different explosion. I'd never seen my grandfather work, except in the old barn where he fixed old cars. Granny Milly never told us the full story, she just always yelled at him and called him a son of a whore.

Sometimes he would have a boat in the old barn that he would fix up; taking months to make sure it was perfect.

When he finished it, the boat would look almost like a new boat, all shiny and brightly painted. Then my grandfather would get drunk, and sell it at the Sand Bar Tavern for a pitiful $25. My granny would be so mad cussing every word she could think of at him. I remember listening to her scream and my grandfather would have a smile on his face, I really think he liked the attention. He would say, *"Now Mama, don't get mad at me!"* that was his pet name for her, and she would eventually forgive him.

Sparks Fly

After a while, I finally got the piano wired up. I took one wire and put it on one end just like I'd seen him do, and then proceeded to do the same to the other end. Then I plugged it into the wall. I didn't even wait to turn it on, but I did however blow every fuse in the house in a matter of seconds!

I heard them running up the stairs, and I knew I was in for it. I was in a great panic by now, trying to get the wires off that stupid old piano, but I'd wrapped them too tight. So I grabbed the piano, and shoved it under my mattress, and sat on the bed just like nothing happened. Even though it wasn't completely dark outside yet, it was still hard to see in my bedroom. If they knew that I had caused the blackout, I think my mother surely would've killed me. So I sat still as a statue not daring to move, my heart pounding in my chest. I think I wasn't even breathing for a moment or 2.

My mother and my older brother Vin came bursting through the door. Both looked almost disappointed that I was sitting there quietly. My mother told me I had to come downstairs until they got the power back on. I asked her if I would be able to go down in a minute, and that I had to put an extra pair of socks on since the floors were so cold (they might as well have been a skating rink, they were like ice). She looked at the window in my bedroom; it already had an inch of ice on the inside as if to confirm the cold for her, she just nodded her head to say yes.

As soon as they left, I didn't even bother to shut the door, panic-stricken at what I had done. I just grabbed that old piano from under the mattress, tore the wires off it, and proceeded to put it back into the top of the closet just as if nothing had happened.

Funny thing was, that was about the only thing I'd never got caught doing. Even so, I was afraid for weeks after that. Even if my mother, or anybody else in the house for that matter, suspected, they could never prove it. I know that if I had not gotten rid of the evidence so quickly, my sister Ann would have found it. I bit the wires off the piano so hard my teeth actually hurt I was afraid to think what would have happened to me if I was caught.

There were a lot of other things that I had hidden all over my room that seemed to be oh- so-important to me as a child. I had homemade Play Doe that we had made in art class. I took it home and made miniature dishes out of it, in all the colors of the rainbow. I had hid them under my mattress for those long days when I was grounded to my room to occupy my mind (stopping me from losing it completely).

Ann eventually found these when she was playing with Minny in our room and they broke them into pieces. I remember crying so hard and feeling completely defeated. I always seemed to get caught. I started to smoke even though it burned my lungs and eyes I had to hide my cigarettes so I wouldn't get caught by mother. I ripped a tiny little hole right in the very center of my mattress. I would take my matches and cigarettes, and hide them in there every night before bed, so I could have a cigarette in the morning on my way to school. My sister was so nosy. I hadn't even had them hidden there for 2 days before she found them.

My mother met me at the end of the driveway. It was horrible, before I knew what was happening, she grabbed me by the hair, and dragged me all the way into the house. my head was on fire from her pulling on my hair and I wasn't even sure what I had done. I sat at the kitchen table too stunned from the pain in my head to even start to apologize for whatever it was that I had done (as I really wasn't sure). Then I saw my two smokes and a book of matches on the kitchen counter. I knew I was in major trouble, even by my high trouble standards.

Sometimes I would just get so sick and tired of begging my mother to stop beating me. It got to the point where it really didn't hurt any more, my skin would just become totally numb. Yet I would beg her, and beg her anyway, because I knew it gave her some sort of sick satisfaction to think that she had that much control over me. The anger inside of me would build and fester. It got so bad that just before I left home for good, I would lie there all night, every night, fantasizing of ways to kill both her and my stepfather. That's when I knew it was time to leave before I did something drastic.

Sick of Smoking

My mother's solution to catching me smoking was to send Vin and Joe up to the store to pick up a package of Export "A" cigarettes. Back in those days it was quite normal to have your kids go buy your smokes. They were the strongest ones you could buy, and they had no filter. She'd also bummed a White Owl cigar off one of the neighbors. I guess she figured if the Exports didn't work in making me quit, she would make me smoke a cigar.

She sat me down at the table, and all the kids gathered around. She opened the package of cigarettes for me, and told me to start smoking. Man was I scared, and really confused. I didn't know whether I should light a cigarette or not, so I told her I didn't want one, and promised her I would quit. She just smashed me across the side the head, and told me to start smoking. So I did.

I was really enjoying myself. This was the coolest thing in the world! So I thought, until after about the 5th cigarette when my stomach started to churn and my head began to spin.

After smoking about half a pack, one right after another, I had to run to the bathroom and throw up. That didn't seem to matter to my mother. She just continued to make me smoke. I was never so sick in all my life.

I finished a whole pack of cigarettes that night in an hour, and swore I would never smoke again. I thought that was my punishment because I was allowed to go to bed, even though I was up most of the night puking my guts out. I must have brushed my teeth a hundred times to get that taste out of my mouth but nothing worked and it wasn't over for me yet. Next morning I woke up for school, and for breakfast I had to smoke that big White Owl cigar, and then walk to school.

My mouth still tasted like a dirty ashtray from the night before. My mother made me inhale every bit of the cigar. I started to have an asthma attack, but she really didn't care. She didn't believe in medication for us kids. So I lived through it and it probably wasn't even a week later that I was smoking again. I threatened Ann with her life if she squealed on me again fear kept her mouth shut my smoking increased to almost a pack a day and I even got bold enough to start going to the old co-op and putting packs of smokes on other peoples account no one ever questioned me and I felt absolutely no guilt in doing it since I was going to hell anyway. Life went on.

***

CHAPTER 6

Mrs. Beasley

My mother was having another one of her foolish fits, as we kids liked to call them. She was yelling and screaming incoherently waking us from our sleep; It was 2 in the morning. She was hovering over us like a monster from a horror movie, screaming at us, *"Get up, get dressed and get the hell out of my house, you spawns of Satan."*

Her blue eyes would be as big as saucers, glowing in the dark it always seemed to me and saliva would hang from the corners of her mouth. Complete terror would be the only way I can use to describe nights like those.

Night Raids

You would think I would have been used to this by now, yet every time it happened (mother going on one of her night rampages), I would shake with fear. I was never able to figure out why she would do this to us. She didn't care if it was minus 40 degrees outside. We had to leave at once and go wait outside in that awful cold. We never wore a jacket, or anything warm for that matter. God, life sucked sometimes back then!

I learned after a while to expect her night raids and kept a turtleneck and a homemade wool sweater under my pillow, just in case I had to get up, and go wait on the step in that awful cold in the dead of the night until her lunatic fit was over. There was no time to get the liners in your boots or put the bags on your feet with the holes in our socks the bags held some warmth even on the coldest days. Every time I touched that homemade sweater, it cut my breath off, but I held onto it anyway every night for fear of freezing to death while standing on the step, waiting.

Sometimes we were outside for 10 minutes, and sometimes for more than 2 hours. It always seemed like a lifetime though. Sometimes we would come in and our rooms would be ripped apart, most of the time though it was just Ann's and mine.

We would then have to go through the beating we always received when she had finished destroying our precious things, and then listen to her ranting and raving. Then we would have to clean our room. By the time we were finished, it would be about 5 or 6 in the morning. There was no point in going to sleep then.

We had a schedule to keep after all. At 6:30 AM on the nose it was rise and shine, time to get the coal and wood in for the day. If we were lucky, it didn't snow the night before. If it snowed, we had to make our way to the barn, and dig out the shovels with our hands. I remember the bitter sting of the snow on my fingers to this day.

Then the massive task began of shoveling a path from the barn to the house began. The snow seemed to fall every single night (or so it seemed to me). It would be piled as high as the telephone poles. The path had to be shoveled quickly to get the wood and coal into the house before the cinders from the fire in the fireplace and warm morning went out from the night before. After this was done, it was time to lug in the 5 gallon buckets of coal, then the wood. It seemed like our toil was never-ending, while she and George sat comfortably warm and drank tea.

I hated him, sitting there with his stocking hat on and a big homemade woolen sweater feeling the warmth from the wood stove in the kitchen as we grew colder by the minute. When we finished, if we didn't have to shovel George out for work or hang the laundry out on the line, we all would sit down for a nice hearty breakfast of ripped-up bread in a bowl with powdered milk and a spoonful of sugar. I really wouldn't have minded if it was real milk, but the smell of that powdered milk made me sick to my stomach and the real milk was saved for mother and George for their morning tea too expensive to be spent on us kids. I tried a few times to go without breakfast, but by mid-afternoon, sitting in school, I would feel so nauseated thinking I was dying from hunger.

This particular night was much worse than other nights, and this time I knew why. It started the day before, when we were woke up at 4 in the morning by my stepfather George. He informed us that our mother was really sick, and she had to be taken to the hospital.

All of us got up and went downstairs to see what was going on. There was my mother, all doubled over, screaming like the devil himself had finally gotten a hold of her rotten soul. Everyone seemed so concerned. But there I was in total glory, thinking that finally the witch was going to get exactly what she deserved! She was going to die, and go straight to hell where she belonged! The ambulance had come to take her to the hospital. As ashamed as I was at the time, I was very happy. Even if she didn't die, maybe they might keep her there for a very long time.

We all got to stay home from school that day, something that never happened. I did begin to worry a bit at this point, thinking mother must be really sick. I watched the parade of phony, overly concerned neighbors coming by the house. They came with food though, so that was somewhat of a good thing. Everyone pretended to be so worried, when really they were all hoping, at least in my mind, that she would die. The, they wouldn't have to have us 4 bastard kids living here dragging down their neighborhood. Divorce was something that just wasn't heard of back then so when mother left her marriage to be with George we were all instantly branded bastards kids born out or their new wedlock.

We waited all day until finally the phone rang. It was the hospital. My mother had apparently gotten food poisoning from a brick of cheese. She told me to take the cheese, and put it in the top of the closet. Someone from the hospital would be over to collect it to do some testing on it.

This was a huge problem for me as I was never allowed to eat cheese. None of us kids were, so I got into the habit of sneaking very small pieces of it whenever I could and this brick of cheese that mother had gotten sick from was no different. I had snuck small slivers of the cheese whenever I could. Until, of course I got the phone call from mother. I took the cheese, and hid it at the top of the closet, waiting with my heart in my throat to get sick like my mother. Then I knew my life would be over. She would kill me. I was eating the forbidden food.

Funny thing was, I never did get sick. Maybe it was from praying so hard. Maybe God was finally having mercy on my soul for being born evil. I was never sure why. Sometimes I used to sit and think about it for hours, and the only thing I could come up with was that God was punishing my mother for all of the hurt she was inflicting upon us kids

A Fiery Farewell to Mrs. Beasley

So that was how it started. When my mother got home from the hospital everything was quiet for about an hour, and then she started. I guess you could call it the calm before the storm. The first thing she did was march Anne and I upstairs, screaming the entire way about how we were the filthiest, little pigs she had ever laid eyes on. Of course she gave us a couple of slaps here and there.

Man, oh man, were we scared! Terrified was more the word I would use! The fear of not knowing is sometimes a lot worse than the fear of knowing. She yelled down to Vin to bring some garbage bags up. I couldn't figure out why. He brought them up like the good boy he always was, or so he thought he was.

My mother continued to yell. We were told to gather up every toy we owned, and put them in the garbage bags. This was fine by me. It was better than a beating. I really thought she was going to throw them out, and I would salvage what I could later. Although it didn't quite play out that way.

We took our toys, every precious one of them, and some of our clothes, the ones we treasured most, like a pair of old patch work jeans I wore every chance that I got.

"Put the bags over your shoulder," my mother instructed us, *"Go down to the fireplace in the living room, and sit on the floor."*

We were never allowed to sit on her furniture for fear we might ruin it even though every piece of furniture in the living room was covered in plastic and had crochet (knitted) blankets on top of the plastic to make them more comfortable I suppose. The thing that happened next will haunt me for the rest of my days, I'm sure. She made us empty our bags of toys and clothes onto the living room floor, then she burned them piece-by-piece. We had to sit and watch as everything we loved and cherished went up the chimney in smoke. I never cried so hard in all my life.

Mrs. Beasley was a very old doll I had for as long as I could remember. I think I loved her because I would talk to her in my darkest moments. I used to think she was really listening to me and understanding. I would comb her silver hair for hours telling her my innermost thoughts. She had killed Mrs. Beasley! That was unforgivable.

Sins of the Step Father

I thought it really couldn't get any worse after that, but somehow as it always was, it did! My stepfather George was in the habit of touching my sister, and I in very intimate places he shouldn't have. George had two daughters of his own who never spoke to him I can't help but wonder if this was the reason why. I didn't know it was wrong, and I'm sure my sister didn't either. Years later when I was in a treatment facility for drug addiction, I confronted her on the issue, but she was in such total denial, that all she would say to me was that she was always afraid to be left home alone with George, but she claimed she never knew why.

If there was an occasion that she was, our mother would always drag her upstairs when she got home, and ask her a million questions.

"What kind of questions?" I asked looking for some sort of validation for my own thoughts.

She never did tell me what kind of questions. It went on for years without my mother knowing. Or maybe she knew, and just didn't want to face up to it. Even when he was caught, she pretended like nothing ever happened. until it came time for mother to leave us alone with George. Then all hell would break loose.

We were sitting on the couch, my stepfather and I, with a blanket over us. He was touching those places he wasn't supposed to touch, when all of the sudden my mother's brother walked into the living room. I think my stepfather pulled himself away quickly or something, but it didn't go unnoticed by my uncle. He went into the kitchen, and I could hear him and my mother arguing. He left shortly after that.

My mother called me upstairs to her room. As per every other day of my existence, I knew I was in trouble. That was the first time I really realized that what George was doing was very wrong. I remember being so afraid because my mother was crying, and I had never seen her cry. She was asking me what had happened, and of course I totally denied it. That is what I had been told to do by George. He said on occasion that if I told anyone, I

54

would be sent away to an orphanage that was run by nuns. He promised that as bad as it was at mother's house the orphanage would be so much worse. Finally, I broke down and told her. As much as I hated my mother, it really bothered me to see her cry.

She took me in the old red car that night to George's sister's house, where I had to tell the whole story over again to Toots, who was George's sister. I stayed there for the night. George had a brother who was a minister, so he flew home the next day to question me and I told him the whole sordid story.

I guess George had prayed for forgiveness, and was given it from the church. I wasn't given a beating for that, but I did suffer every time my mother left us alone with him. He never really did stop either. As time went on, he would tell me, and probably my sister also, that he would kill me if anything were ever said again to mother or anyone else. It was a very sad and scary place for me living in that fear all the time. I was so afraid after that, I just took the beatings my mother gave me, and swore I would never breathe a word.

I guess because mother was in the hospital (for what didn't seem nearly long enough to me) she just assumed we were all upstairs having a big sex orgy. To be honest with you that was probably the one and only time I remember my stepfather didn't try any hanky panky on my sister or me. We still got a beating for it anyway, per ritual at this point.

I don't think I had ever seen her as angry as that night. To this day, I swear she was foaming at the mouth. This is where it got so bad I have a hard time fitting it into my memory. I wonder whether my mother was really that evil, or did I just imagine it.

It was about 3:30 in the afternoon. All of the toys and clothes had been burnt, including my beloved Mrs. Beasley. I had carefully hidden her in the back of my closet for so long always afraid this moment would come and mother would take Mrs. Beasley away from me. I was sure she had possessed some magical power to keep the devil away from me.

My mother said, "Let's go for a drive." I could feel the terror welling up inside of me as I slowly put my shoes on. My mother was constantly taking us out for a drive, telling us how much she despised us, and how she would like to just drop us off somewhere.

Sometimes she would actually make us get out of the car and watch her as she drove off. She would usually go for about an hour, or sometimes a bit more. We would sit there and cry. She was pretty sneaky about it too. She always did it on a dark, deserted road, where she was sure there wasn't going to be any traffic. So no one was ever there to help us. It was usually out around old Broughton Road.

Town of Broughton

Broughton was an old abandoned town that was rumored to be haunted by the people that used to live there in the town before it died out. There were a lot of stories about whole families that had disappeared while driving down those old dirt roads. I couldn't understand why she would drop us off there in the middle of nowhere, because she had her own little scare there awhile back. You see her and my stepfather would like to go for long drives, or that's what we thought.

I guess one night while George and her were out there on that dark deserted road, doing whatever it was that they did when they went parking. George thought he heard something in the woods. My mother panicked, and begged him not to get out of the car, but he went anyway. He wasn't gone for very long when she heard his ungodly scream. He came running back to the car as if he had seen a ghost, he was so white.

"Shut the doors," he screamed. *"Start the car."*

I guess at this point my mother knew something was up. At that moment she looked up. There was a man running toward them with an axe in his hand. Just as they were backing up, he came down with the axe and smashed it right into the hood of the car. We were still up when they got home, and got to hear the whole story as they told it to the R.C.M.P. (Royal Canadian Mounted Police).

The police officer said it was probably just a "moonshiner". They had probably scared him as much as he had scared them. I went to bed that night, terrified that the person would recognize the car, and come hunting for them. They never did catch the guy, nor did my mother and George ever go parking after that. That kind of sucked! It was really the only peace I had ever had (when both of them were gone).

Butterscotch Palace

She would take me out sometimes by myself, and just terrify me. We would be heading into Sydney, and she would always stop at the nut house, us kids called it the butterscotch palace, either on the way there, or on the way back. She would make me get out of the car, and stand right at the front doors. Then she would proceed to tell me that this is where I belonged, and she had a good mind to leave me there. She would drive a few feet and then stop, laughing all the time as I begged her not to leave me.

Sheer terror is what I felt every time she did this. I would see those people with their helmets on, through the front windows, sitting there either staring off into space or banging their heads over and over against the walls.

This day however was different, I could sense it. It seemed like the drive to Sydney took forever. I knew this time we weren't going for a shopping trip. The cupboards were full, and of course there was no money for new clothes. I knew what was in store for me, even if no words were spoken about it. The closer we drove, the more my anxiety grew. I knew once and for all, my mother would be rid of me.

We went to our usual spot at the front doors. The funny thing was, terrified as I was, I thought in the back of my mind, these nuts were way saner than the mother I was living with! This time my mother did something different though. She didn't jump in the car, drive away, and laugh, like she usually did as I followed along crying. This time she rang the bell, and stood there silently waiting for someone to come and answer the door.

When someone finally came to answer the door, to my disappointment, my mother politely asked them to give us a tour of the place. I remember the nurse (or whatever she was), stating that it was against regulations to let anyone in unless it was a family member, or a group on a tour. My mother politely told her she was a leader of the Canadian Girl Guides of Canada, which she was, and she wanted to see if the place was suitable for a tour. Well, how could this person argue? It was potential business. How mom got into the Girl Guides is still beyond me.

Although I still felt really apprehensive about the whole thing, my nervousness was almost gone during the tour. I was starting to think my mother had lost her touch!

"Is this all she has to scare me with?" I laughed to myself.

I was so busy looking in the room where they gave the shock treatment, I didn't notice that my mother and the nurse had slipped away. This was her whole plan from the start.

I panicked, running down those dark halls, watching people drool all over themselves, or worse, coming toward me with a helmet on their heads, with that blank and vacant zombie look in their eyes. It seemed like I ran forever, but finally I reached a nurse's station.

I asked them in between gasping for breaths where my mother was. I was politely told she was sick of me running off, so she had gone to the car to wait. Boy, did they look mad at me, but I got the point from my mother. I got it loud and clear. After our little outing, I went home and went to bed. That's when the night raid began.

***

CHAPTER 7

Claire

The wind was blowing so hard today, you could almost feel the spirits in the air. It was a very uneasy feeling in the pit of my guts like something wasn't right. I was finally off my grounding, which was the umpteenth dozenth time I had been grounded this year. I had nowhere to go. Everyone I hung out with was either up at the co-op hanging out, or was doing homework. I was never allowed to hang out at the co-op even though it was the store the whole town went to for their basic needs. It was forbidden by both mother and George I was only allowed to go for mother to get what was needed and then head straight back home.

It was no wonder I always felt like I didn't quite fit in there (or anywhere else for that matter). That's where all the slutty girls, and dope smoking boys went to hang out and get into trouble, according to my mother. The girls that went to hang out in front of the co-op were there for one thing and one thing only. The bad boys were there to collect on that one thing. I really wasn't sure what that one thing was at the time, but later on I found out it was sex. What a dirty little word. It was a word I dared not use back then or I would have gotten my mouth washed out with soap. Sometimes even today, I have a hard time saying the big"S" word silly as it seems. Some memories are just burned into your brain for an eternity it seems.

I decided to go upstairs and do some reading since there was nothing else to do. Mind you, I liked to read, no I actually loved to read. It was the one thing that took me to such far away wonderful places where nothing or no one could touch me or hurt me in any way. I spent a lot of time at the library. As much time as mother allowed me to go actually.

There was nothing better, than a good story to help you forget about all of your problems.

One of the few things I treasured most in my childhood that my mother could never take away from me was my membership to the library. I don't think it ever occurred to mother how much I enjoyed reading; I am sure though if she knew how much I had enjoyed it, she surely would have banned me from going there ever. It really seemed to bother her when I enjoyed anything, or maybe I was just so consumed with hate that this was my way of thinking.

I headed up to the bedroom to lose myself in one of the wonderful stories. It was a bit chilly, so I crawled under the covers, laid my head on the pillow, and started to read.

Forerunners

I woke up in my grandmother's house totally confused. There were a lot of people there, standing around crying. Everything seemed totally unreal. I looked around at everybody for a few minutes. I don't know if I was trying to figure out how I got there, or why everyone was crying.

Then suddenly I noticed it. There in the living room was a casket. You see, where I come from you never went to a funeral home to bury someone. You always had their wake in the living room. It was some kind of superstition where you had to lay them out in the living room, cover the mirrors, and open all of the windows. This was so their soul could escape to heaven and not end up trapped in the house.

I didn't know who it was in the casket so I slowly walked closer. To my horror the closer I got the more I realized that it was my brother Joe. *"No it can't be!"* I yelled.

I had my hand out as if to shake him but it seemed to take forever to walk the 10 or so feet across the living room floor. As I got closer I realized his back was facing everyone, but I was so sure it was him.

Finally, after what seemed like an eternity, I touched his shoulder. To my horror, he rolled over. I let out a scream that sounded foreign even to my own ears. The face that greeted me was not my brother's. However, it was that of my cousin Claire.

Claire was not really my cousin but an uncle. We were however very close in age. The average family size back then was about 15 kids. Sometimes more than 15 but very rarely less than 15 per family. Usually by the time the oldest child in a family got married or pregnant (at about 15 or 16 years old) their mothers were still having babies. This left huge age gaps from oldest to youngest in families. Seems almost crazy today that people were allowed to marry so young, but it was just so normal in the towns that lined the coast of our small island that no one ever questioned it.

So my aunts and uncles were so close in age to me we all just considered ourselves cousins. Claire was 14, just a few years older than me. When we went to see granny Milly on Sundays he was always there with a half a dozen other kids. His parents were actually my God parents Charlie and Luigia, although I didn't really see too much of them except on holidays like Christmas. Being a godparent back really only meant if mother was to die I would go live with them and they would look after me. Out of all of the kids that were always at granny Millie's on Sundays, I had to say Claire was one of my favorites with his dashing smile and his long curly blond hair we always seem to have so much fun as he was full of adventure.

It seemed to me his deep blue eyes were always smiling. He got a gift for his 14th birthday, it was a dirt bike. *"Top of the line"* was what Claire told all of us kids when he drove it to Granny Millie's that day. Oh how I wanted to ride it! Claire said *"No!"*, that it was too dangerous for little girls. He raced up and down the old dirt roads all day that Sunday and I heard granny Milly mutters under her breath that this was no good and that that bike would be the death of him. A shiver of fear ran right through me when I heard those words escape Granny Millie's' lips.

Suddenly, I felt an ice-cold wetness that sent a shock right through my body. I realized it was just a dream. But what a dream! It had really scared me. The ice-cold wetness was of course my mother waking me up in her usual fashion for supper with a wonderful plastic cup filled with ice cold water from the tap. I wasn't sure if I should tell anyone about the dream but to me it had just seemed so real.

Granma Linster came for supper that night. How I loved to sit and listen to her sometimes. Tonight however, I was in no mood for what she had to say, but I would have gotten a really good whack if I dared to interrupt. I wasn't interested. That was, until she said something to catch my attention.

"Have you talked to Granny Milly?" she asked my mother. *"No,"* was the short reply. That was a forbidden subject in our house. Since the last incident, no one dared speak of Granny Milly.

"Well," continued my Granma Linster, *"She told me she and all the kids were sitting at the table for supper last night, when all of the sudden the big mirror in the hall came crashing down, and shattered into a million pieces. No one was even around it. You know what that means don't you?"*

All of us kids were just sitting there, open-mouthed because we knew what it meant. Someone was going to die. Who it was we had no idea. No one was sick that we knew of. My mother was in quite a state of shock, and for one of those very few times, I had seen her at a loss for words. My mother chose to close the subject by getting up, and asking my Granma to come help her with gathering all of the stuff she had made for the craft sale. Nothing more was mentioned that night, or at least not in front of us kids.

Past Lives

When I went to bed that night I dreamed the same dream that I had dreamed that night before supper. There was one other dream I continued to have throughout my childhood, and what a strange dream it was. In my dream, I was always a small boy. I'm not sure what year it was, but the clothes I wore were very distinctive to me. They seemed like old clothes from somewhere in England, in the 1800's. In my dream, my brother Joe and I were church robbers. I never really could remember much of the dream, just the running part.

You see, we would always be spotted just as we were on our way out of the church. I don't think we were stealing much, just wine to sell at the local market, but it was always the same dream, and we would always get caught. After we were caught, there would be a trial, and we would be sentenced to be buried alive in a concrete tomb. It was always the same dream, with always the same results. Funny thing is, I still think about that dream to this day. I sometimes think it has something to do with a past life of some sorts.

I woke up the next morning to hear my mother talking to someone on the phone. I couldn't believe that I had actually woke up before I was half drowned with that ice cold water. It sounded like a pretty serious conversation, so I figured I better get my butt moving before she started my day off with one of her rages. I couldn't help but stop and listen as I headed down the stairs. My mother was on the phone talking to someone about some dream that they had the night before. Curiosity got the better of me as I listened to her say good bye, and start to dial someone else.

I knew I would be in big trouble if I was caught, but I just couldn't help myself. She was
talking about my dream! How could she know? Suddenly, I realized that I wasn't the only one who had that awful dream about Joe, who wasn't really

64

Joe, but Claire. Quickly I got dressed, and went to the porch to stack the wood for the day's fire, straining my ears trying to find out what was going on. It didn't take long either.

My mother and George were sitting having their morning tea when us kids were finally finished, and sat down for our usual breakfast. We all heard them talking about how Cat and Granny Milly had the same dream the night before. As my mother described it to George, I felt the blood draining from my face. It was the exact dream I had, right down to the clock being stopped on the wall at 8:35AM.

You see, when there was a death in our family, the clock on Granny Millie's wall always stopped. No one ever knew why, it just did. My mother looked over at me just before I fainted, and asked something, but I really had no idea what it was she said.

The next thing I remember was waking up on the floor, soaked. For once it wasn't from water being thrown on my face. It was actually sweat. I was quite frightened. Nothing like that had ever happened to me. I think my mother was a bit afraid too, because I got to go watch television instead of finishing the morning chores. I wouldn't dare tell anyone my dream for fear of facing my mother's wrath.

After I felt a bit better, I got up and went to school as usual. I guess it was about 11:30 in the morning when all of us kids got called into the office.

"You need to go home immediately." was all that we were told by the principal, Mr. Howley. Fearing the worst, we all quickly grabbed our homework for that night, and ran all the way home.

When we got there, my mother informed us that there had been a terrible accident, and we all had to go to Granny Millie's at once. We were smart enough not to ask any questions, and just quietly got into the car. I was shocked to see the scene when we arrived. There were people everywhere. Finally we were led out of the darkness, and into the light.

My cousin Claire had been driving his dirt bike along the beach with his friends that morning before school. It was time to go home and get ready for school. Claire told his friends that he needed to go back to the beach. *"Why?"* they had asked him. But he couldn't give them an answer. All he had said was he knew he had to go back, and there was no way he could go

home. So they had left him there, and went on their way. Once they arrived at school, they got called into the office by the principal. Granny Milly was on the phone, wondering where Claire was.

The boys told her they had left him at the beach, explaining that he had refused to come with them. By this time, my Granny had been in a panic, partly from the dream the night before, and partly because Claire would never miss one of Granny's hot breakfasts. So, she had called the police and went to the beach to look for him herself.

Thank God she didn't find him. The police did. I think it probably would have killed her. I guess he had been driving along the sand dunes, and hit a hole. There had been ice on top of it, so he had probably thought he could drive right over it but that wasn't the case. The ice had broken through and his front tire got stuck in it, sending him over the handle bars and breaking

his neck.

It was a sad day. He was only 14 years old. I swear I saw my granny age 10 years right before my very eyes that day. So that's why we had all had the dream, a forerunner is what they are called, when you see something that will happen before it actually happens. I wouldn't dare tell my mother that I had the same dream. God only knows what would have happened to me.

The wake was exactly like I had dreamed it, right down to my brother's clothes, because he was the only one who owned an old hand me down suit, and that's what they buried Claire in. I looked up at the wake and looked at the clock on the wall. It was stopped at 8:35 a.m., the exact time he had died. Life would never be the same without Claire.

***

CHAPTER 8

Wish Upon a Star

Once the funeral was over, my Granny Milly and my mother started talking again. Boy did I miss my Granny! All was well for a while. What I mean by that was that nothing really stands out in my mind, so I just assumed everything was well.

<u>My Best Friend</u>

Then, my sister Ann and I were on our way home from school one day. A big German Shepherd dog came out of nowhere, and proceeded to follow us home. This was not good. If a strange dog followed you home back then, it was a sure sign that it would bring bad luck, not only for you, but for everyone else around you (especially if it was a black dog). Another superstition imposed upon us as children. This dog wasn't black, but he did have some black on him. He was prominently brown with a white stripe going right through from the tip of his nose to the top of his head, so it was still bad luck all the same.

Try as we might, we could not get rid of that dog. We stopped every few steps to yell at him to go away but he just refused to leave us alone. Not that he was scary, or cross, or anything like that, because he wasn't, it was just really bad to bring a stray dog home.

Both my sister and I knew what kind of a beating we would get if we didn't get rid of that dog. We tried everything. We jumped fences only to find the dog on the other side once we got over. We went into our friend's (Karrie Dawn) house and snuck through the back door, but that stupid dog was still there!

Kerry Dawn's mother, Marge, was the town's hairdresser and Kerry was a part of our little gang that hung out whenever we could. Marge did everyone's hair in our small town and that meant that everyone looked exactly the same! All of the women had heads like poodles short all the way around and permed on the top. All of the young girls looked like she had put a bowl over their head and had cut around it to shape their hair like a bowl. Oh, how mother hated her, why I was never really sure.

One time in fact the only time she ever sent me there for a haircut I came home looking like the rest of the girls and was promptly sent right back as mother screamed at her on the phone about how my hair needed to be short because I was unable to look after it myself. I was embarrassed when I got there but it was nothing compared to the embarrassment that I felt when I left. It was so awful and short I looked just like a 10 year old boy.

Finally, we decided to try to stop and talk to the dog, and try to make him understand. Believe it or not, I think he actually did. We sat on the curb out of sight from our house, and politely told this dog of our dilemma. How we would get a good beating, and he would probably be shot if he continued to follow us home. I really think the stupid dog understood, because he just sat there as we left and made our way home. That wasn't the last we were to see of that dog though.

As soon as we got home, the insanity began once again. My mother was ranting and raving about one thing or another. We had learned at a young age to be very apologetic for things, even for things we didn't do, especially when she was on one of her rants. Funny, everyday single day my sister and I would walk home from school, it was about a 10 minute walk from the school to our house. Just as soon as I would round the corner onto the street just before our street and sure enough I would have to go to the bathroom and I could not hold it no matter how I tried.

I think it was the fear of not knowing what to expect when I got home that triggered this reaction. I would hurry into the bushes and relieve myself feeling better if only for a moment. The problem was that every single time someone seemed to see me and call mother to tell her I was peeing outside again. Then, of course I would get a good beating but still I did not learn.

A Sty in the Eye

I did the same thing every day for years when I was on my way home. I would then lie and swear up and down I didn't do it but in the end I always got caught. Then of course there was or is probably still today an old superstition that goes if you get caught pissing on the wrong side of the road you would get a sty on your eye. It seemed to me as sure as I am sitting here every time I used the bathroom outside and lied about it I would wake up with a sty on my eye and mother could then see my guilt.

Even if no one had seen me, I would always wake up the next morning with a sty on my eye and mother would know I had once again done the most unforgivable thing and peed outside. In those days I think everything we did was an unforgivable sin. In later years, I found out that sties were generally caused by eyelashes falling into your eyes when you were sleeping, but at that time I was convinced that it was God's way of punishing me for being born evil and all. When I did wake up in those mornings, trying my best not to rub the terrible pain away from my eye, my mother was always so... maybe "kind" is the word I'm looking for. She would take her wedding ring off and make the cross 3 times on my eye lid, and it really did seem to work. It was only afterward, when the pain started to subside, that she would beat me all over the kitchen.

After a while though, I got a lot smarter and claimed the pain was really bad right up
until it was time to go to school so I wouldn't get the beating I knew would eventually come. It was a dangerous game I played. I always knew when I got home the beating would be 10 times worse because she had all day to stew in her anger, but I didn't care. It was better than going

70

to school so sore I couldn't move. I have no idea why we were in trouble that day, but we were as usual.

We were just about to get a good beating, when that damn stray dog popped up again. George was out talking to the SPCA (Society for Prevention of Cruelty to Animals); they were always around picking up stray dogs because there were so many of them. I guess George had seen them put the dog that tried to follow us home in their dogcatcher truck. George then asked them who owned the dog, considering we lived in a small community someone had to own him. No one had ever seen the dog before according to the man. He said he had asked around before deciding to take the dog into custody. George decided at that moment to take the dog home. Mother wasn't too impressed but George was determined to keep him.

The dog catcher warned him that the dog was part wolf, and could turn on him or us kids
at any time, but George took him in anyway. The first thing on the agenda was what to call this half bred dog that was part German Shepherd and part wolf. We all came up with the name,
Star, after our favorite television show; Starsky and Hutch.

Sometimes I swear that dog was part human. He seemed to know what we were talking
about. He even knew his name the minute we called him by it. He a great dog! No one knew where he had come from, but he was completely trained. He never once had an accident in the house. He was loyal, did all of the tricks you would ask him to do, and as a bonus he would let us dress him up in old dresses we had hanging in the closet. The best part was when he would obediently sit on my old banana seat bike, and let me double ride him all around the neighborhood to show him off. It was probably one of the best

times of my life. Sadly, those times though were not meant to last. Before all was said and done my precious Star would be gone forever.

The Clubhouse

I guess it all started innocently enough, with Andrew Read coming down to our house from his farm, complaining about Star stealing his chickens. There was another dog in the neighborhood though, that all of us kids suspected at first. Her name was Sheba. She was part husky and a part wolf. We were all pretty sure it was her, so we didn't put too much thought into it at first. Pretty soon however, we noticed Star would leave in the mornings and not come back until supper time. Then one of the neighbors called our house, saying that they had seen a pack of dogs, just like a wolf pack, running through the woods around Andrew's house. Star was the leader of the pack. This was very scary for me. I was so afraid to lose my dog. So, I came up with a plan to fix that old coot, Andrew.

Me and my plans as a kid, I don't think ever once did I have one that actually worked out. But this one seemed like the perfect plan. With the help of my friends, we had built a small cabin in the woods. Well, not really a cabin, just a bunch of old trees stacked in a circle. It was what we called our clubhouse, a place where we made all of our silly little plans and had all of our big dreams that we had all hoped one day would come true. It was also a place where I could run and escape to when I felt like I couldn't take any more of my mother and stepfather.

The day I realized I was going to lose my precious dog Star, I began my journey into one of the most evil places a little girl can go in her mind: I was going to burn that old bastard's house to the ground! I believed that would save my beloved Star. There was no way I was going to let anyone take my dog from me. He was not just my dog, but my protector against all things I had considered evil, like mother.

Every time my mother went to beat one of us kids, Star would freak out and jump in front of us to protect us. It would take every last ounce of her strength to drag him outside. I think

Star had a sense of what was going to happen to us. By the time she would get him outside, she would be exhausted. She used to beat him too, with logs from the stove, the broom, or whatever else she could get her hands on.

He would just take the beating for us. There could never be another dog to replace him. So now you see why I loved him so much. I set my plan into action, never breathing a word to anyone. I waited for about 2 weeks to put my plan into effect, all the while, the knot of fear growing in my stomach, worrying that they would come and take my precious dog and protector away. They didn't, though they threatened too many times. It was getting cold out, so I knew it was all going to work out perfectly.

The Pot Boiled Over

I woke up one day, and decided that today was the day, the day to fix that old bastard Andrew Read once and for all for trying to take away my dog. I got out of bed despite the chill that always went right through to my bones in those awful winters. Funny thing was, it was only late October. The winters were so damn long there.

Anyway, I got up got out of bed, did my usual chores, all the while praying and doing everything twice to make sure I didn't get into trouble. I swear I felt sick the whole time. I am not sure if it was the excitement of following through with my plan. Maybe it was the fear of my evil mother looking into my eyes and knowing that I was really carrying out Satan's work, just like she had always expected me to.

So finally I was finished, ready to get the club members together and launch stage one of my plan. The first thing I did was to call everybody, and tell them we had to have an emergency club meeting. I told them something had happened at the club house. They didn't know that I had snuck up to the club house the night before and destroyed it. It really did break my heart, for you see this was my safe place. I began to destroy it piece by piece, at least as much as my heart would allow. The one and only place I could ever go and dream, dream of those freedoms that always seemed just within my grasp, but yet so far out of reach. As much as it hurt me to destroy my only safe place I knew, I did not have any choice in the matter.

The love of that dog was much stronger than any place I could ever escape to. After things were destroyed, I sat for a few minutes and shed a few tears for the loss of my second home, then went on my way as if nothing had happened. I guess, after a while of getting the snot beaten out of you, over and over again because you were crying, you learn to hide and mask your emotions pretty well.

Those people who have been there know what I am talking about, when I say you just stuff it until one day when you've had enough, the pot finally boils over. I probably felt somewhat guilty (as much as someone who was the seed of Satan could of course!). I went home that night, and acted as though nothing was going on, answered my mother's endless questions, then went off to bed. I was even surprised I could sleep that night, but I did. The excitement was too much for my little mind to handle.

With my plan well under way, I called the emergency meeting and showed everyone the terrible things that had been done to our little clubhouse. We were all in agreement that it was no longer safe to have it there and something had to be done. We had to move our secret location and never return to those woods.

Everyone was in agreement. So we all headed toward the shore. Once we were about half way there, I suddenly remembered (or at least that was what I told everyone) that I had forgotten the attendance book. I could never leave that behind. No one even knew about the secret club.

As I put it to the girls that day, *"Can you imagine if the wrong person got a hold of it?"*

Those were the writings of our journey through this thing we called life. There would be no way we would ever possibly live it down. Someone offered to go with me, but I quickly responded that whoever did this might be waiting, and ready to follow whoever it is that came around. I, after all, knew these woods intimately, and could very easily lose someone, so therefore it would be much safer for me to go on my own. I was impressed; my plan for once was actually working much better than I had thought it would!

I told the girls to scout out the woods around us, and that I wouldn't be long. Just like I said, I knew the woods better than probably anyone in that whole godforsaken town, so I ran up the road a bit until everyone was out of sight, and quickly slipped into the small path I had made to cut my time in half (to get back to where the destroyed club was).

Fire in the Woods

When I finally reached my destination, I didn't have time to sit, even though I was gasping for breath. I quickly took our precious attendance book, and used it to start the fire. I had planned carefully, almost too carefully. I set the book on fire, and without thinking, tossed it into the heap of dried wood. I swear, it was not like a fire more like an explosion. I almost didn't have time to make my escape. I think I might have panicked, but my fear of getting caught would never allow me to do that.

As quickly as I could, I made my way back to the other girls, who fired a million questions at me all at once. They could all see the fire. It was like the whole town was burning down. They however did not suspect me, of course. I wasn't gone for that long, even though to me it seemed like a thousand life times. You could feel the panic in the air, so I called everyone to attention, and told them that if we were to run into anyone, we would not breathe a word.

What if the whole forest burned down? That was the one big question everyone seemed to ask over and over. As for me, I really didn't care. You see, the club was positioned right next to that bastard's field. It was always referred to as Andrew Reid's field. Even though I didn't plan this when I had started with my little spot, it really could not have been any more perfect. I could only hope Andrew and his whole rotten family would burn to the ground, along with
their stupid farm house.

I could really see their point though. We all felt the same way. As much as we hated our town, this little spot in hell (as we liked to call it) it was, after all, the only thing we had ever known. Sure, I remember the places I was before, but it was like living in a trap here. After a while, I really started to believe that those other places I had lived in were only figments of
my imagination.

So, we all pinky swore, and started up the long road to home, swearing not to breathe a word to a single soul. However, on this day, luck was not on our side. Once we hit the long dirt road we called the Shore Road, we could see a figure in the distance. Panic was completely starting to set in by now within the whole group. What if whoever it was knew that I was the last?
person seen at the club? No one really knew what to do, and it was actually Sherry (a friend of my sisters') who suggested that we run toward whoever it was. The idea was to pretend like
we had just been at the shore looking for lobsters when we saw the woods on fire. That was the quickest decision ever made by any of us in the club.

There was no debate or argument. We all started running toward the distant figure at once. The closer I got, I began to realize that it was the neighbor, Lloyd and my heart began to feel a bit lighter and freer. I knew in my heart that even if he thought or suspected anything, he would never say a word.

I still covered all of my bases after the fact though, just to be sure. We all ran up to Lloyd yelling and screaming as if our lives depended on it, quickly telling him the terrible made-up story we had planned to tell him. I was sure he knew the awful truth however, the way that he looked at me. It was almost like he could see the evil flowing from my tiny, little wicked veins.

He did however, rush down with us to the site of the fire to help put it out. I was never so afraid in all of my life, nor had I ever seen someone work so fast. I was terrified that he was going to suggest calling the fire department, but thank God he didn't. The fire that looked so enormous to us kids was put out by him grabbing a large log and continually beating it to pieces on the ground until it was almost extinguished. Then he proceeded to yell at all of us to go scrape as much dirt and gravel from the road as we could to kill the remainder of it. We did this so quickly and obediently I don't think any one of us had a thought in our mind except sheer terror. I thought, deep down, the club members would surely tell on me, but they were afraid of the evil inside me. No one breathed a word, no matter how many questions that Lloyd asked. So we were safe for the time being. Rather, "I" was safe. However, that was not the end of this sordid story.... That's what you get for playing with fire.

***

CHAPTER 9

Gordie

Soon after the fire in the woods, I began to get this itch inside my soul. An emptiness that just never seemed to go away. There was something about getting away with setting that fire that was so exciting to me. I mean, sure I got into many fights at school, but sometimes I felt almost guilty about it. The whole fighting thing, bullying people was because I was just so rageful inside. This feeling however, was not a guilty feeling at all though. What I really did feel was a feeling of personal satisfaction.

Soul Sickness

It was such a great feeling that I started to look for something, (anything, really) else to give me that same feeling it was like a soul sickness deep inside of my being. I realize what that feeling is now that I am much older. There was an emptiness inside of me that in another person would have normally been filled by the love of a mother and a father. I did not get that love, something I realized much later on, so naturally I had to look for other ways to fill that large aching gap inside of me. I wish I knew then what I

know now! But I didn't... so on with the story.

I swear, at first I tried so hard to bury that feeling of emptiness, but it just kept growing no matter how hard or what I tried. It grew so large, in fact, that I thought in my messed-up mind that it would eventually swallow me whole if I didn't find or create something to fill it. So I began to try everything to get that feeling back, but nothing worked.

What did I try, you might ask? First and foremost was fighting. God, I was such a bully! When I think back now, most people (especially

78

the kids I had hung out with) were only friendly to me out of fear. Fear that I was coming after them. To kick the crap out of them, for some imaginary reason, something they did or didn't do that I had created in my own sick and twisted mind.

Now I know. I can now see what they could see at the time, shameful as it was. They saw

the anger on the outside and not the ball of rage, hatred and fear inside of me that would fester more and more as every day went by. It wasn't their fault. I just needed attention. Any kind of attention is always better than none, right? I was so desperate for someone to pay some kind of attention to me.

Soon, after fighting every day 3 times a day for about a week, I realized that the empty pit in my stomach just got bigger. Until, one day I was on my way to the store when I ran into Gordie and his gang.

The Bully

A long time ago, when we first moved to that God awful place, Gordie was the leader. Not anymore. I came in, and little by little, began to take over his territory. First, I had to face the utmost challenge, and beat the living hell out of him. Funny I say it that way, as if it was so easy. It was definitely one of the hardest things I ever had to do.

I remember it clearly like it was yesterday, how it all came about. It started the very first day we moved in, when my mother sent me to the Co-Op alone. Not really thinking anything of it, I jumped on my bike, eager to get away from the awful chore of unpacking. Once I got to the store, there was a whole gang of kids. I didn't think anything of it. I jumped off my bike with a friendly smile, expecting to make a lot of new friends. To my surprise, it didn't happen that way at all.

First they surrounded me and Gordie proceeded to tell me that if I wanted to enter the store, I would have to either pay a quarter or fight. I was terrified. I knew I could not give him the quarter. I would get the beating of my life when I got home. My mother accounted for every penny. Gordie was the bully back then. I knew that I could never fight him, partly because I was a big wimp, and partly because I knew, or I thought I knew, he would kill me.

So, I did the unspeakable. I just stood there and cried like a baby. I cried until finally Gerald, the store owner, noticed me, and came to rescue me. Once inside, I called my mother, crying my eyes out, begging her to come get me. Finally, after what seemed like forever I could see her car coming up the road. Feeling a little bit braver, I stuck my head out the door to brag that my mother was coming and that all of those rotten kids were going to go to jail.

They could see the car too and quickly began to scatter in all directions. I swear if it hadn't been for Gerald backing my story, my mother would have beaten me silly for wasting her time. I did get a few slaps though, but nothing I couldn't handle. This went on for a couple of months. Every time I left the house, I was terrified. I would always call my mother, and she would come to get me. Unfortunately, the beatings got a lot worse. She beat me harder for continually wasting her time. I really didn't care, for the beatings were better than facing Gordie.

Street Credit

Then one fine sunny day, it was the same as usual, yet it wasn't. My mother sent me
to the store to get one thing or another. There was the whole gang of them waiting for me. That same oh-so-familiar knot of fear welled up inside of me, making me feel like I was going to either crap my pants or puke (I was never sure which one). That day however, after being terrified as usual, I called my mother. She basically told me she was sick and tired of me being such a sucky baby. I would have to find my own way out of it.

80

I really could not believe it. At first I was speechless. Really! I mean, what the hell was I supposed to do? As much as I begged and pleaded with her, she would not come and get me. So there I was, left on my own to face the thing I feared the most (besides my mother, of course). I stayed in the store for about a half hour until my mother called, and threatened me with drastic

measures that I knew she could and would carry out.

I knew I was done for, so I slowly opened the door and looked at the crowd of kids gathering around. Suddenly, I wasn't scared anymore, I was angry. No, anger is an understatement. I was enraged! I did something that was totally out of character for me. I marched right up to that bully, Gordie, grabbed him by the scruff of his neck, and proceeded to pound the living crap out of him. Believe me, I was just as shocked as anyone there, but that was the best thing I ever did in that little town. I took out the toughest, meanest bully, and gained all

kinds of respect and street credit, that day.

That was the beginning of my days as the tough guy (never mind that I was a girl!). From that day on, I was the bully, the one waiting for people after school every day just to beat them up. Of course, I didn't realize I was trying to fill that hole in the pit of my stomach. Mind you, it really did seem to work at first, now that I think about it. After a while, I just did it to be a showoff, so people would look at me, but even that only worked for a while. When I think back now, I spent so much time looking for "the" next thing to fill the emptiness. I think I kind of lost myself, or maybe I never really knew who I was to begin with.

Temporary Fix

I clearly remember another day, running into Gordie and his gang. As soon as I walked up to them, I knew something was up. I just wasn't sure what it was. To me they looked kind of funny, even from a distance. The closer I got, I soon figured it out. They were all drunk.

"Where in the hell did you get the booze?" was the first question I asked as soon as I was within earshot.

I think Gordie could hear the envy in my voice, so he pretended not to hear me at first. I was about to get peeved, but realized if I did, it would ruin all chances of my getting any of their stash. Instead of pulling my usual stunts to be the center of attention, I calmly walked over to them and asked the question once again. Not wanting to say anything in front of everyone there, they motioned me to come around to the back of the post office, into the nearby field. This was actually pretty smart for a bunch of drunken kids.

Of course I followed them. I could almost taste the booze, even though I had only had a few mouthfuls in my entire life. I think even way back then, I was an alcoholic. We got to the tall grass, which was supposed to be their cabin, at which I used to laugh at constantly. They were all laughing.

"Do you see it?" Gordie asked.

"What?" I replied.

No sooner were the words out of my mouth, I noticed that there in front of me were

4 bottles of wine. I couldn't believe my eyes! I thought I had died and gone to heaven.

"Where the hell did you get these?!" I yelled.

At first they weren't going to tell me, but I seemed to have quite a way of persuading people when I wanted to.

"From the church." was Gordy's reply.

I swear to God, I felt like I needed to go crap myself the minute it came out of his mouth.

I knew I had found some thing to fill that hole because it was suddenly gone. First I thought it was the booze. I sat and drank, not really caring about the consequences for the first time in my life. Then it suddenly dawned on me. It wasn't the booze! It was the excitement of what they had done

Break And Enter

I know it sounds really screwed up. The more they talked with that excitement in their voices about breaking into the church and stealing the wine, the more I felt like I was about to be doing what I was meant to do. Agreeing to go back with them made me feel invincible.

After downing 2 bottles of that precious wine, we got up and headed up the hill to perform our dirty deed. I mean what the heck, I was going to hell anyway, or so I thought. I really had nothing to lose. Mind you, that was only how I felt back then. I would never disrespect God in that way today. Not because of fear of going to hell, but out of pure respect and complete understanding that I am not going to hell

As we headed up the hill, our excitement and fear grew, until I had myself so worked up, I puked right there in the middle of the road. I know it wasn't from the wine, but the adrenaline. Once we got to the top of the hill, the half mile walk to the church seemed to take a lifetime. I was so close to chickening out. But what would happen to my status as one of the town bullies if I did?

So as scared shitless as I was, I just kept going, even though every fiber in my body was screaming, and telling me, *"This is so wrong!"* Amazingly, I still feel a lot of guilt over this, even today. When we approached the church, I did exactly as I was instructed. They left the back door open. I just had to go in, and grab the wine from the cabinet under the back curtain in the basement.

It wasn't until we were in that they told me about the money stash. They made it sound so simple. All we had to do was break the lock on the office door, and we could have all kinds of cash. This was where they supposedly kept the weekly offerings from all of us sinners. I was never a greedy person, and I felt such a terrible guilt about our plan, but I agreed to do it anyway just to fit in, and be a part of the group, peer pressure will do that. Thinking quickly, I told the boys that I would grab the wine, and go hide it outside while they tried to figure a way into the office. Not thinking anything of it, they all quickly agreed.

I think I was really good at playing the tough guy back then. As quickly as I could, I gathered up the remaining 3 bottles of wine, and made a very quick exit. I really considered not even going back into the church, but how would I explain that one?

As usual, I had a plan. I tossed the wine under a couple of bushes and ran back into the church, probably looking as scared as I felt. I told Gordie and his gang that someone had seen me coming out of the church doors, and slowed down to see what was going on. This was the best plan I could come up with. It really did make perfect sense because we lived in such a small and nosey community. They believed me of course, and we all made a mad dash for the woods. It was such a rush of adrenaline that I don't know if the emptiness was gone, but I certainly wasn't feeling it right then and there!

That was it, the beginning of the end. I loved that sick feeling that I was going to puke and crap at the same time, that feeling of invincibility like I was untouchable. Now that I knew what gave me that feeling, I began to do all sorts of nutty things trying to get it back. Like every addiction/dependency, each time it had to be just a little bit more. Eventually, it could never be enough, no matter how much I did or tried to do. It's strange how now I realize the one thing that

84

was missing, and could have filled that sad, empty feeling inside of me, was me. Unfortunately, it took me way too many years to realize it. This was not the end of my dealings with Gordie.

***

CHAPTER 10

Mary

I really thought in my mind that I had taken care of that old coot Andrew Read, but that was not to be the case. I thought for sure he had seen the fire I had set, and knowing somehow it was me, and that I meant business, he would surely back off. He didn't see the fire. In fact he wasn't even home that fateful day that was to set my destiny. Man, was I peeved! As a matter

of fact, because we had all each sworn each other to secrecy and Lloyd was never the type

to cause trouble, nothing was ever said about the fire, even to this day.

<u>"Star" of the Neighborhood</u>

So Andrew didn't get the message I had hoped he would, and things started to go downhill from there. I swear sometimes, it seemed like every day there was a new complaint from one of the neighbors about my precious dog Star. I think that even still today, because we lived in such a small community, everyone talked and began to gang up against my dog. Calls came in from everyone.

Even when Star was in the house for the day, he was still accused of doing nasty stuff. No amount of argument could convince the community that it wasn't him. I was so afraid, so very afraid all the time that they were going to come and take him away. That dog gave me all the love of 10 parents, never mind the negative ones I had! As more complaints came about him and what he was or wasn't doing, the more violent and aggressive I became acting out every chance I got. When I would listen to my mother and George talking, I would become sick with worry.

We always heard from the time we were knee high to a grasshopper that children should be seen and not heard. God help you if you got caught listening to adult conversations. To be honest though, I really didn't care if I was caught or what the consequences would be for listening. That's how much I loved that dog. If it was a parent calling, I was always sure to catch who it was, so I could beat the crap out of their kid or kids the next day, thinking this would

dissuade their parents from calling up with stories that were so not true.

There was even an old woman who called, and I got wind of it. Mary, I think her name was. She was so old; I swear she made it up just so people would know she was still alive. No one had ever seen her leave the house. They said she had some kind of phobia, and was afraid to go outside.

I was sitting in the kitchen when she called and she must have been liking the conversations she was having with mother because she began to call every day. She always started with a complaint about my dog then proceeded to talk on forever about anything and everything under the sun. As my mother talked to her using her sweetest, most sickening voice, I could feel the hatred and rage build. I had to leave the kitchen for fear that my fantasy of stabbing my mother to death was about to come true. I knew I had to do something but I just

wasn't sure what.

<u>Contrary with Mary</u>

Finally, after a few days I came to a decision. I would get my gang together and threaten Mary. How we were going to do this, I wasn't sure, but I did know I would figure out a way. It took a lot of persuasion on my part, and some threatening, but I got everyone together so we could come up with a plan. They all knew how I felt about my beloved dog Star. We talked for what seemed like hours at that meeting, but could not come up with some way to scare the old bat, Mary.

Then like something out of the movie *"The Outsiders"*, came Gordie and his gang. No one in our group would dare to call him over, except me of course. They were all terrified of him, and what he might do to them if he were crossed.

I, however, had already proven my point as a tough guy even though I was a girl, so I had nothing to fear. I told everybody to relax, and climbed out of the elephant ears (which was our temporary club until I could find something better). I think Gordie almost sensed what we needed him for, because he was a lot cockier than usual, if that was even possible. We told him of our dilemma, or at least the parts he needed to know, but nothing about why we were doing it.

He could never think we would be that weak over some old, dumb dog. I couldn't believe my luck. He was related to the old bat, Mary, and informed us that once a month his mother took her out for groceries. Rain or shine, they went out on the same day every month. As pure luck would have it, the day they were to go out was only 2 days away! So we sat there for a bit longer, and hatched our plans to do something awful to her.

Only 2 days later, I showed up at her house with my sister, just like we had planned. The problem was, we were the only ones that showed up! My sister, Ann was very afraid, and just pretended we never made any plans. Hell, she even suggested that we lie, and say we were there. No one would know, right? But I would know. I was peeved. There was no chance in hell I was backing out, no matter what. So, feeling sorry for her, I told her to go hide in the long grass, and keep an eye out for anyone who might come by.

She did as she was told, not out of loyalty though, more out of fear of the torture I would put her through if she didn't obey, I was quite a tyrant! I went through the bathroom window. It was open just as Gordie said it would be. I was driven by adrenaline, love for Star, hate, anger and fear (all at the same time if that's possible). I had never done anything so wrong or so daring in my entire short life.

Haunted House

Once I got in the house, I completely froze. Something would not let me leave that bathroom no matter how hard I tried. At first I thought it was fear, but then I could feel a man on the other side of the door, even though everyone including Gordie swore to me that she lived alone. I found out a later that her husband had died in the room next to the bathroom. I swear to this day, it was him that I could feel, or should I say the ghost of him. Just as I am also sure that if I hadn't been so afraid to open my eyes, I would have seen him there looming over me, threatening me for invading his house.

Even though it seemed like an eternity I was in that haunted house, it was probably only about 10 minutes. I didn't do anything while I was in there. I'm not even sure if I breathed! I was too afraid of what might be waiting for me on the other side of the door.

When I did crawl back out through the window into my familiar surroundings to go and get my sister, I was surprised to see that she was no longer alone. There was Gordie and his merry band of misfits, waiting to see if I was really going to do what I had promised I would.
Being the tough guy, I instantly started to brag about how I had trashed the old bag's house, so that for sure she would get the message to butt out.

We all took off like bats out of hell running for anywhere but there. I felt the pure rush of adrenaline running through my veins and I loved it! I was on top of the world for just a brief moment in time. I didn't even care at the time if anyone ever found out what I did. Once I returned home, I realized with a sinking heart that they would surely take my Star away. I had not yet done what I had set out to do and that was stop them from taking the only thing in this world away from me that really mattered, my dog Star.

All of the kids sat for the next few days waiting in eager anticipation to see if anything would be said about the supposed hell I had called down upon Mary. I just sat with them letting their imaginations go wild, not ever even thinking about letting them know what a chicken I really was. A few of the kids started to poke around after a bit, wondering why nothing was said or why the cops weren't called to investigate.

I guess that's when the rumors started about her place being haunted. It was then that I heard the story about her husband of 50 years dying of cancer, and swearing on his death bed to always be there to protect her. When I heard this, it sent chills up my spine. I knew he had been there. Boy oh boy, did that scare me! Of course, I could not say a word, even though all of the kids were amazed that I had not encountered his spirit. Little did they know.

Spring Fever

Then one day out of the blue, when I thought I could not take another insane moment. An idea came to me. It sounded even too good for my ears. Mary was the driving force in trying to get rid of my Star. It was springtime by now. All of the flowers and apple blossoms were out. I always loved this time of year, when my soul felt alive. Maybe it was because the winters were so long and hard, I'm not sure.

Somehow, spring always made me kind of crazy, "spring fever" is what it is often referred to even to this day. A time when people fell in love and some people went crazy after being penned up inside all winter with no fresh air.

I unfortunately was and still am one of those people who just go crazy. You could start to pick the first crab apples off of the trees. Mind you, they weren't very big, only about the size of a nickel. They were perfect though, perfect enough for my plan. I really think all of us kids got a touch of spring fever every year. I'm not sure if the rest got it as badly as I did, but

I had decided that since I was too afraid to go back into that house with the old man's ghost, I would retaliate from the outside. I swear that I never thought about the consequences or

maybe I did, and was just so desperate that I really didn't care.

Pay Back

We all had homemade sling shots in those days; even though they were forbidden after one of the kids actually lost an eye. We were all smart enough to keep them hidden. We made them with small tree branches we cut trees that were in the shape of a Y. With about a million elastics tied together, we tied both ends of the branch. It was the time of the year when you couldn't find any spare elastic bands in our small town. Besides, who would even notice the bruises? So I slowly and carefully, picked out a few accomplices that would be able to carry out my task with me. I took them aside, one by one, and told them of my plan. Funny, now I think about it, they were all in agreement, but the only one dumb enough to stand beside me was my sister Ann, as usual.

The day finally came. It was Saturday morning at 9 AM exactly. We were all to meet outside the old bag (Mary's) house, and man, was she going to get hers! Of course there was a problem. No one else showed up! Chickens, that's what they were all of them! So I basically forced my sister into my life of crime that day, and told her she had 2 options, be with me, or against me. She didn't have much of a choice, or her life would have been so bad. Mind you, I would have still protected her from the bullies, but I was, after all, the biggest bully of them all.

We began our dirty deed, first playing "Nicky, Nicky nine doors", to get Mary's attention. The minute she peaked her head out of that front room window curtain, we began to terrorize her. We belted one crab apple after another at her house with our home made sling shots, hoping to break some of her windows. As much as we tried though, they only dented the siding but never broke through any of the windows. To this day, I swear it was her dead husband that would not let us near her.

Then something happened that I will never forget. Her husband came out the front door! That's right, her husband! If it weren't for my sister being right there beside me, I swear I thought I'd finally lost my mind. There was that old bat, Mary, with a sick look of satisfaction on her face as my sister and I stood there too terrified to move, or even scream.

Finally, after what seemed like an eternity, standing there watching him slowly walk down the steps toward us, we both ran like the devil himself was chasing us. As we were running, we could hear her on her front porch, laughing like a witch from some very scary horror movie. I will never forget Mary!

When we got home, all hell was breaking lose. Little did we know that we were the cause of it, or at least it took us about 30 seconds of getting our hair ripped out to realize it. That was the way my mother always worked. She would beat the living crap out of you first, and then if she felt like it later on, she would sit down to ask you what had happened. Funny, even then she would tell us we were filthy little liars, and beat the crap out of us again.

A Beating to Remember

I guess Mary had made some calls while my sister and I were running for our lives, telling all of the parents of our plan. How she found out was the real puzzling part for everyone, not just us. Of course she lied, and told all the adults that we were so stupid, we made the plans right outside her window. This was so far from the truth that it wasn't even funny. I knew that none of the kids would dare tell her, and I also knew it wasn't one of my mother's tricks, because the phone was ringing nonstop with angry parents.

My mother was raging so badly, that even poor Star would not dare get in her way. I knew my sister and I were really in for a good one. I had actually felt a bit sorry for my sister, and told my mother that the whole plan was my idea. I was a lot tougher than my sister, so I figured I could take it. If only I had known how severe the beating would get!

The first thing she did was pull out the belt. Mind you, the belt I could handle as long as it was only applied to my butt. This time, however, was a lot different. She gave us the strap (belt) like we used to get in school, but not on the palm of the hands like the principal would do. She hit the back of my sister's hands, then all over her body. I started to cry just watching. I knew that as bad as my sister was getting it, I was going to get it 10 times worse. This was of course because I was the ring leader. That was my mother's justification.

I remember clearly during the beating, thinking about a book I had once read about a young boy who didn't have nerve endings, and could not feel any pain no matter how hard he was beaten. God, how I wished that was me that day! By the time she was done with me, I was hardly able to move, but the bruises and swelling had not yet started, so the second part of our nightmare was about to begin.

Mother told my sister and me to get our shoes on, and to go get into the car. I was always terrified when she did this. I never knew what her sick mind was thinking, but we did not dare refuse her. God only knows, she might actually kill us. I remember her telling us from time to time about how young girls would disappear, and no one would ever ask any questions. They would just assume the girl was in the family way, and had to go live in one of those homes for wayward girls.

Being in the family way was about the biggest shame even though everyone had kids in our home town and all across the island for that matter by the time they were 16 once you got pregnant you were forced into marriage and if no one came forward as the father of your child you were sent away to a private place where nuns lived give birth and the baby would be taken immediately to be put up for adoption never to be mentioned by the family again sad it was when I think of it now .

The most famous maternity home was in East Chester Nova Scotia, owned and operated by William and Lila young. He was a chiropractor and Lila was a midwife who presented herself as a doctor, they were tried for various crimes in their home including manslaughter.

The house promised both maternity care for local married couples and discreet birthing and placement for babies of unwed mothers. The home was all about illegal trade of babies between Canada and the United States. The Young's it was later discovered would purposely starve the unmarketable babies by feeding them only molasses and water. The poor babies only usually lasted two weeks. Once the babies died their bodies were disposed of in small wooded grocery boxes that were typically used for dairy products. They were termed butter box babies and many of their bodies were either buried on the property or burnt in the old coal furnace.

That was mothers way of threatening us without actually coming right out and saying it. So we reluctantly did as we were told, fearing the worst all the while. The worst we feared, however, was nothing compared to what she was about to make us do.

House of Horrors

"You little tramps are going down to that poor old woman's house and apologize to her." were the first words out of her mouth before the car was even started. My sister started to wail almost to the point of hysterics. As for myself, I just sat there, silent tears rolling down my face, too afraid to even speak. The closer we got to Mary's house, the more hysterical my sister became, until I could see my mother's face start to contort, which is what it did always just before she started to rage.

I think my sister saw it too, because all of a sudden, she was talking so calmly, it was like she had become a different person. She told my mother of the incident that happened with old Mary's husband first coming out of the house, and then coming down the steps.

"Is this true?" my mother asked me. I was so afraid of admitting it, and being called a filthy little liar, but I was way more afraid of going to that house and maybe having the ghost of that old man try to possess my soul.

"Yes." I said. It was barely a whisper, I'm not even sure if my mother or sister had actually heard me.

Even though it was only a short drive to Mary's house, it seemed like an eternity for me. All the while I was hoping my mother would show some kind of mercy (for the first time in her miserable life) on her 2 children who were just unfortunate products of their dysfunctional environment. Of course, she didn't. She kept right on going.

I think she was really enjoying our terror, until we got there. I began to realize that what we had told her must have scared her too, though she would never admit it. She refused to get out of the car, although old Mary was waving her up with all her might.

What could we do? My sister and I were in a hopeless situation. There was Mary, and then there was our mother. If we stayed in the car, (the thought did briefly cross my mind), we were going to get it even worse when we got home. If we were to get out of the car, and go up the steps, we were taking a chance of being possessed by the old man's ghost. I swear time stood still for me that day as I waited for my sister to make a move first, even though I was the older one.

I was sitting in the back, thank God. My mother reached over my sister, yanked the door opened, and gave her such a shove. It sent her flying about 2 feet out of the car! I didn't even wait for my mother to turn around. I was gone out of the car, and on my way to face whatever was to assail me at

95

the top of those steps. My sister and I clung to each other, terrified, as we made the long and dreadful climb up to the front door.

Old Mary answered the door just like she wasn't expecting us at all. I was thinking to myself, what does she think we are, stupid or senile? We had seen her trying to wave my mother into the house.

"Come in, come in." she said to my sister and me as we got closer.

"Um, um, no." we both said at the same time. *"We... ah... just came to say..."*

She interrupted us again with her *"Come in. Come in."*

"No." I said, much more firmly this time. I was really quite surprised at how small and frail she looked up close.

She wasn't that much bigger than I was, and I was only 3 feet 11.

Poison Pie

"Wait one minute." she said, and without waiting for our reply, she quickly disappeared into the house. My heart was in my throat. I literally started to gag out of fear, not knowing why she would leave us out there. I think she was enjoying our fear way too much. Finally she was back. *"Are you sure you won't come in?"* she asked for what seemed like the 100th time.

"No." was our answer once again.

"We just came to say how sorry we are for throwing crab apples at your house."

"Was that you?" she asked. I could not believe my ears.

"Yes, and we are so sorry." both my sister and I told her.

"Well no mind, dears. Here is an apple pie!" I almost laughed at the irony of it all. Us throwing crab apples at her house and Mary giving us a pie made with those very same apples!

"Take it home and enjoy it."

"No, that's ok." we both almost yelled at her.

96

"I insist." she said.

There was something in her underlying tone that made me reach out and grab it, even though my whole body and being was screaming against it. Funny, she didn't get angry, or even tell us not to do it again. She just went into the house, closed the door and locked it. I think she was the only person I ever met in that small town that actually had a lock on her door.

I wish with all my heart that my mother had turned her head that day, because I would

have accidently dropped that pie. I thought, no I knew, it had some kind of poison in it! Just like I knew my mother would probably make us eat it, hoping it would get rid of us once and for all.

Once we got home, however, my mother completely ignored us. She made a bee line for the phone, calling people to tell them of what we had done. Both my sister and I breathed a sigh of relief. I had to go lay down. The pain was getting really bad from the vicious beating I received earlier.

I wasn't laying down for long when my mother came upstairs to wake me up. As hard as I tried to hear her, especially in the mornings, it was no use. I just slept like a dead person.

I was very surprised I didn't wake up in the usual fashion, with that God awful cup of icy cold water thrown in my face.

Deformed Stranger

When I think back now, I guess my face was really frighteningly disfigured from the beating I received earlier that day. I must say, that was one of the very few times in my life that I saw that memorable expression on my mother's face. I guess it somewhat resembled fear, when I think about it now. Way back then, it just puzzled me. I could not for the life of me figure out what that look was, but I spent many a night sleepless, wondering. I guess what they say is true, with age comes wisdom.

God, I must have looked horrible. That was the one and only time my mother, in my short unhappy life, did not pressure me to get out of bed. She just looked at me with that weird expression on her face, and without saying a word, shut the door and left. I knew instantly something was wrong, and boy, oh boy, was I afraid of what it might be. I thought maybe my mother had permanently disfigured me in some way.

That was the reason why she wasn't beating me right at that very moment for not getting up on time. I really wasn't in the habit of looking in the mirror admiring myself as much as I was accused of it. Vanity was a sin, and I already had enough sins against me. I was like the red headed stepchild, like I fell out of the ugly tree, and hit every branch on the way down. At least
that's how I saw myself.

I mustered up enough strength and courage to get up, and go look for myself. I was horrified. Now I could understand why my mother had just looked at me and shut the door. My face was so swollen, I really wasn't even sure if it was really me in that mirror. It was like looking at some hideously deformed stranger. I was so horrified, I started to cry.

That's when I realized that my hands were so swollen; I could not even grab a small piece of toilet paper to wipe the never-ending tears streaming down my face. My mother came bursting into the bathroom, completely ignoring the state I was in, and informed me that I was to stay in my room. Under no circumstances was I to leave unless I had her permission. I dared not disobey her, so I slowly made my way back to my room.

I was so grateful for the solace of my room. I actually felt ashamed for what I looked like, thinking in my childish mind I had done something to deserve it. Mind you, what I had done was wrong, but in no way did I deserve what had happened to me. I lay peacefully in my bed, and for the first time in my life, cursed God for not saving me. I wished I would just die and put an end to this tortuous life.

Room Sanctuary

Then the dreams came. Ah, those wonderful dreams! They were always the same, but I loved them. Dreams of freedom that made my soul ache like it never ached before. I'm not sure
how long I was in that state, for I was sleeping and dreaming. I wished it would never end. I guess that was long before the nightmares started.

My food was brought to me in my room, so I have no idea how much time had actually passed before I started to come to. My mother had apparently told the school that I had fallen ill, and I was very near death's door, in the hospital. There was a lot of speculation from our strange little community, that I had eaten the (poisoned) pie from old Mary. How people ever found
out about that pie, I'm not sure, but I suspect my mother had something to do with starting the rumors.

I don't know how long I was in that dreamy state of mind. The whole class got together, and sent me a bunch of stuff, kind of like a Care package. It must have been like that for a while, a couple of week's maybe. I rather enjoyed having stuff brought to me, even though I was in pain. As I think back now, I realize that the vicious beating had given me that little bit of attention that my soul so desperately cried out for. It was a very surreal experience for me, living between fantasy and reality.

My, oh my, how I did enjoy it! I think it was the longest time I had ever gone without getting a beating. My mother was probably afraid that if she hit me any further, she might do some irreparable damage. Little did she know, she had done that on a daily basis to my emotional body. This time it was my physical body. The fog was finally starting to clear in my brain, when something happened to start a ball rolling, that no matter how much I tried, I could not stop.

***

Chapter 11
Moon Mullins

My sister, Ann, came tearing into the house late one afternoon. She was supposed to be out playing with her friends, storming in through the door like the devil himself had possessed her. I had been in bed for about a week or more at this point still somewhat recovering from the mother of all beatings mother had laid on me.

The Day a Star Lost His Glitter

I could hear her screaming downstairs so incoherently, I had to really strain to hear what all the fuss was about. I learned pretty quickly though as I sat my pain-filled, battered and bruised body up to strain to hear through the closed door and hear it I did. Much to my dismay, Star was in the fight of his life with a black Labrador retriever named Smokey.

The whole street was trying to break it up by the time my sister got home. It was bad. There was blood everywhere. Eventually my stepfather and the other dog's owner had to beat them apart with clothes' props (those things you prop the clothes lines up with). We didn't have the convenience of dryers back then, everyone hung their clothes out winter, summer, rain or shine.

Someone even called the animal control to see if there was any way they could come and take away my dog before he attacked and killed a kid, was the words they used.

Eventually they did break the 2 dogs apart, but Star came out of the fight with only one ear. Of course, we couldn't take him to the vet. After all, we were poor. There was no money for things like that. My step father brought home our poor, battered dog, and we tried as best we could to patch him up. Something happened to Star after that fateful day. He was never the same. I think his mind finally snapped. Maybe it was from taking too many beatings for us to protect us from mother, or maybe he just knew his days were numbered.

On my very first day out after my so-called "hospitalization" (I say hospitalization because that's what mother had told the whole town as to where I had been for the last few weeks); mother had decided to take Ann and me to town. She also decided to take Star, which was very unusual. My mother hated this animal, our protector. I think maybe she sensed something in him about his changed state of mind that I as a child, was not able to. I did my usual ritual of kissing Star on the head as I always did before I had to part with him (sometimes I kissed him even if I just had to go to get the clothes in off the line). Before we went into the grocery store, the walk was painful through the grocery store as I was still not quite healed up completely from the beating.

Wolf Pack

We weren't in there long, when someone came up to my mother and asked her if she owned the old red car in the parking lot. She replied, *"Yes why, is there something wrong?"* They quickly informed her she better get out there in a hurry.

When we reached the car mother running ahead of us, I will never forget the sight that awaited us. Star had gone absolutely nuts in the short time we had been inside the store. He had completely ripped apart every inch of the interior. Not only did he rip it apart he ate most of it or so it seemed to me from looking at it. There was nothing left but a few strands of cloth hanging from the inside roof, and a lot of metal.

There was quite a crowd gathering around our old red car, staring in total awe and disbelief. I was even a little bit afraid to open the car door, but my mother had no other choice. I think I secretly hoped that Star would chew her apart the way he had done the car. That was not the case. My mother jumped to one side as she flung the door open. Immediately, Star stopped his shredding, and wagged his tail like nothing had happened. I was shocked!

We drove home with Star. I kept rubbing his beautiful coat, telling him everything was going to be all right even though I knew in my heart of hearts it wouldn't be. Nothing would ever be the same again for both my precious dog and myself. I prayed so hard that day to a God, I wasn't even sure existed. I was begging and pleading with him so that no one would take my only understanding friend away. In my heart, I knew the God I was taught to fear wasn't listening, or maybe he was too busy trying to save the starving kids to have time for my precious Star.

The closer we got to home, the more I felt I couldn't breathe, waiting for the inevitable to happen. Surprisingly, it didn't. All was quiet while my mother and stepfather whispered in the kitchen, while all of us kids strained our ears to hear even though children should be seen and not heard. I think they were both in a state of shock.

After a day or 2, it was decided that Star would be taken to a farm where he could run free. Star was, according to my stepfather, (which I give him credit for to this day) much too smart to have his life ended. Star would be kept on a leash in the yard until a suitable home was found for him.

Star was wild however. It was in his blood just like me and he was half wolf after all. Even thick chains could not keep him tied up. He always found a way out of them, and then out of our yard, into danger. It seems like it all happened in a blur my biggest fear and worse nightmare coming true all at the same time. Star escaped once again. My brother, Joe was sent to look for him. We could hear Joe screaming well before he got to our house.

A Final Farewell to Star

At first we thought that someone had been shot or run over, but it was Star once again. He was leading his pack of dogs around town as usual; the dogs seemed to follow him whenever he was off his leash. It was as George would often say when he saw it, "The way of the wolves". Even though none of the other dogs were wolves they still had that powerful innate animal instinct.

The dog pack, or should I say just Star, got into a fight with a poor little hound dog. He literally ripped that dog apart, killing it right on the owner's door step. When he was done the dirty deed, he proceeded to drag the remains down the steps and eat it. The rest of his pack joined in the feast.

That was the end of my precious Star's life that night. My mother and stepfather packed him into the car, not even caring to lie to us about what they were doing. It was time for him to go. They said it could have been one of us kids, but I don't think Star would have been capable of doing such a thing to one of us. We had an understanding. Our goodbye was hard, and still hurts to think about it to this day, but I knew I could do no more to save my dog. It was time to let go.

They took him from my grasp as silent tears streamed down my face, and led him to his ultimate fate. Moon Mullins a farmer that lived a few miles up the road put a bullet in him for the price of a pint of whisky.

***

Chapter 12

Freedom

After Star's death, I got a whole lot angrier. Every fiber of my being screamed hate. Hate for everything and hate for every single person I came into contact with. I began such a reign of terror in our little town, that no one was safe, not even my poor sister, Ann.

<u>Venting The Wrong Way</u>

One day, not a few weeks after the whole incident, she was sitting on the floor, drinking a glass of orange juice. She was minding her own business, but in my mind, I thought she was taunting me. Man, did this make me angry! As I was walking by her, I just snapped. I swear it was like my foot wasn't even my own. It was almost like some strong outside force had taken control of it. Before I knew what was happening, or was able to even think about stopping it, my foot flew up and kicked her square in the face.

Orange juice went flying everywhere, and my sister sat there in shock. I burst
out laughing. To me, this was one of the funniest things I had ever seen. My mother however, did not think it was so funny, and almost on cue, out came the belt.

There seemed to be a different person living inside of my body at that point. Even that leather belt didn't keep me from smiling with pleasure at what I had done. Ann had an orange ring around her nose and lips for weeks afterwards. Every time I would look at her, I would start to snicker, and have to leave the room for fear of my mother's wrath.

I seemed to be almost lost to myself at this point, sometimes not even caring anymore about my mother and all of her insanity. I remember just asking God every single day, *"why?"* Why did God and my mother hate me so much? Why did God hate me, and more importantly, what had I done to deserve this? Why was he not sending someone to help me, when I prayed every night for him to do just that? Maybe they were all right. Maybe I was just born evil!

I was rebelling at this point, not only outside of our house, but inside as well. There didn't seem to be any end to this torturous life, so I figured what is the point? I was, after all, always being accused of being the bad seed, so I might as well fulfill my destiny. I felt as though I was to be doomed here to this hell forever.

My sister got the worst of my anger for a while in the weeks that followed. One time in particular stands out. It was dish time. We always had to do the dishes, and I hated every miserable minute of it.

Dishing it Out

If the dishes weren't done to my mother's specifications, or if there was one speck of food, or even dust for that matter, look out. My nutty mother would strip everything out of the cupboards, pots, pans, plates, cups and whatever else was in there, all the while ranting and raving about us *"ungrateful little bastards."* Then she would grab both my sister and I by the hair from wherever we were, drag us down to the sink, and we would have to re-wash everything. I think she did this a lot on the days when she was bored, or when she couldn't find anything else to blame us for on that particular day.

Ann always liked to antagonize me when we were doing the dishes. Alas, that didn't help. This one day, my sister was in an especially aggravating mood, so every dish I washed, she would give me that stupid grin of hers, then throw it back into the sink. I was reaching the end of my

106

(admittedly short) rope very quickly. Mimicking mother, she would say it was still dirty. I would give her a slight kick in the shin, tell her it wasn't dirty, and throw it back into her sink. This lasted for quite a few dishes. We were just getting to the last of them when we happened upon a spoon.

This is something my sister and I still laugh about to this day. Once again the argument ensued, her saying it was dirty, and then I would say it wasn't. Realizing she was not going to win the argument and seeing that she was getting the best of me, my sister called to my mother. This infuriated me to no end.

As she was screaming about the dirty spoon which, I will admit, was in fact dirty, I slowly and carefully began to fill the dirty spaghetti pot up with icy cold water. I could hear my mother coming down the stairs. I figured I was in for it anyway, so without a second thought, I took the huge pot, and dumped the whole thing right over my sister's head.

What a mess! I started to laugh so hard, I almost peed myself right there on the kitchen floor. The look on my sister's face was priceless! There was water everywhere, but I didn't care. I think my mother must have thought it quite funny too. I didn't get a beating nearly as bad as what I thought it would be.

Life went on, and eventually the hurt over my dog went from a sharp sting in my chest to a dull ache. I was finally able to gain a little bit of control over my rage and anger. What really helped me tremendously in those days were my dreams. Dreams of that beautiful freedom. I started dreaming about another escape. This one as far as I was concerned, would not fail. What I was going to do or how I was going to do it. I wasn't too sure. Thinking about it put a little bit of

lightness into my soul. I must have come up with a million plans, but alas, I was just a big chicken inside. Sometimes I was so afraid of being caught, that I was afraid to even think about my plan, never mind carry it out.

So, I secretly and quietly just dreamed those dreams of freedoms that were to come. I was always very careful not to let out my joy in the slightest way for fear mother might get wind of it and maybe take me back to the butterscotch palace where she could lock me up and forget about me like the rest of the crazies.

**

CHAPTER 13

Mrs. Hobbs

In our little town, they say that death happens in 3's. From all the evidence from my years on this earth, I really and truly believe it. This day started out like any other day, beautiful and sunny. It was a Sunday. I know this because we always went to see Granny Milly on Sunday. There we were, getting ready to go for our usual Sunday visit, when Vin asked if we could all go to the show.

"No," my mother said in one of her nice voices, explaining to Vin that she didn't have the money. I wished that she would talk to me that nicely sometimes, but that would never happen. As soon as Vin mentioned the show, I got a real funny feeling in the pit of my stomach. Years later, I would identify that feeling as pure fear. Sure, I had felt fear before, but this was a different kind of fear. It was a fear for someone else's life.

Let me explain from the beginning. Even as we all piled into the car to head up to Granny Millie's, I still couldn't shake that feeling. I was (much too soon) going to find out why. All of the kids were home when we got there, waiting around patiently to see if we would all get that one little pleasure of going to Olive's show.

The show was such a big deal back then. It was like a little slice of heaven. It cost 25 cents to get in, and the snacks were so cheap, not like today. A bag of chips was only 10 cents. For a nickel, you could get either a huge strip of fizz candy, or 3 long red licorices. We usually got 35 cents each. Boy, did we think we were on top of the world! Sometimes we would get really lucky.

My grandpa would be home, and then we were guaranteed an extra dime each. Sometimes he would pass the dimes out so quickly; it was like he was a magician usually pulling them from behind our ear. Not one of us kids ever saw what the other was getting. He was always a fair man, never treating any one of us better than the other. We would quickly take our small fortune, and hide it in our sock, squealing with delight the whole time, so afraid of being caught.

Granny Linsters Visions

On this particular day my mother had no money, so I was doubtful that we would go anywhere. To my surprise, Granny Milly was digging through her big black purse as we all came piling in through the door. She was more than willing to pay for all of us to go have a little bit of fun. She was just about to start handing out quarters, when Granny Linster came bursting in like a tornado.

"Do not send those kids anywhere today!" she was yelling, even before she got the old porch door completely opened.

Granny Linster had a forerunner that was an omen, sign, or indication that something was about to happen and that something was usually a death of some kind. The feeling in the pit of my stomach that I had all day long grew so much bigger at that moment.

At first, no one was even able to make out her rambling.

"I have seen it. I have seen it was all!" she kept yelling.

Finally, after a lot of convincing from Granny Milly, she was able sit, and calm down a bit, enough for us to get the story out of her.

So Granny Linster began one of her infamous tales of the future. She had a dream... or a vision. I am not sure, even to this day, what the difference is. Her ability to have dreams that were glimpses of the future was something I had inherited from her (but didn't know it at the time). The only difference was that her second sight was accepted by the whole family.

110

I was just a seed of Satan in my (and their) own eyes. It seemed that way, but not by my Granny Milly, or anyone else in the family, because they had no idea at this point that I also had been born with the gift. "Seers" is the name folks would use for someone like Granny Linster, she was considered to be a person endowed with profound moral and spiritual insight or knowledge; a wise person or sage who possessed intuitive powers. I was so afraid to come forward because of my certifiably crazy mother and lecherous stepfather. I am not sure if anyone else even knew.

Granny Linster began to speak. We all sat on the edge of our seats, as usual. She apparently had gone home last night after church, (she went to church every single night) stoked up the fire, and sat down to read the Bible. At some point she had fallen asleep.

Something woke her abruptly (or at least she thought it had). She had such a questioning look on her face while recalling this. I don't think she really knew. She heard a commotion out the window. In her dream-waking state, she got up to see what was happening. What she saw, she said quite frankly turned a couple of her almost-grey hairs white.

She was terrified of what she was witnessing outside her front window. There were fire trucks and police cars everywhere. In her mind's eye, she could see the old post office, even though her house was nowhere near it. There was such a huge crowd gathered around that she knew something was going on that was very wrong. Try as she might, she could not crane her neck so she could see past the crowd.

She came rushing over to Granny Millie's house the minute church got out the next day, to be reassured that none of us kids would be going up past the old post office that day. I remember her words so clearly to this day. She said that something very evil lingered around there that day. To say we were frightened was an understatement.

We all loved our Granny Linster, and most of what she told us usually happened, or was just about to happen. I remember many times going up to Granny Millie's house and getting so excited knowing that Granny Linster was coming. She would sit us all around the table, and tell us the most frightening stories we had ever heard. We were scared out of our wits, but yet could not pull ourselves away from the table, even to use the bathroom.

Granny Linster was from Newfoundland, a place famous for its stories of ghosts and hauntings. We would all sit intently and listen, afraid that we might not get every little bit of the story. When she was sure that she had scared us enough, she would point her bony finger at us and send us all up the stairs. My Granny Milly and my mother would never say a word until afterward (when we were all too terrified to go to bed).

Then they would be furious at her. She had experienced another one of her visions. As she sat down to tell us, I could see a dark cloud forming around every one of us in that house. That day, there would be no little bit of fun we usually had to break up a very hard week. All thoughts of it was gone right out the window with the story Granny Linster was about to tell us. I was so disappointed, sitting outside on the old swing, rocking back and forth, wondering to myself what in the world I was going to do now.

Not a Stocking of a Lie

Suddenly, like a flash, I decided I was not going to take the advice Granny Linster handed out so freely. I would not heed her so-called warning. I was going to find a way to go to that show if it killed me. Pippi Long Stocking was playing and it was one of the very few shows I had not seen. It sounded so simple. All I would need was some money, and someone stupid enough to go with me!

Then I remembered my grandfather was up in the old barn working on a boat or a car. He was always working on some old hunk of junk as

112

Granny Milly called them. I knew if he had no idea what was going on, I thought if I could get to him before he heard anything, he would definitely give me the money I needed to carry out my crafty (and fun) plan. He was always very generous with all of us kids, even when he didn't have what we were asking for. If it was money, candy or whatever else, he would always find a way to get it for us.

Still wondering who I could get to go on my little adventure with me, there in the distance I could see the one person I knew in the world I could talk into anything, Minny. My mood instantly lightened. I almost laughed to myself. She was, after all, not the sharpest knife in the drawer!

It was a bit harder than I thought it would be to convince her, but after a few minutes she finally caved. We headed up to the old barn to scam some money off my grandfather. We didn't have to tell him what we needed it for. All we ever had to do was ask. He would never ask why.

We made up some stupid story anyway, looked him in the face, and
lied. I was very good
at lying, so I had been told over and over again by my mother.
"If you were standing on a stack of bibles, and swearing to the truth, I still wouldn't
believe you." she would always tell me.

We told my grandfather we had to go to the store for Granny Milly for some bogus errand. I don't remember what, but he never suspected a thing. I felt really guilty for a long time after that. He blamed himself for giving us the money after the incident happened. I never lied to him after that time. The guilt I felt after that day was just too overwhelming.

We ended up getting 50 cents each from my grandfather that day which was a lot of money considering it was usually a quarter from mother and another dime from Granny Milly and that would buy us more than we needed at the show. I sent Minny into the house to tell Granny Milly and my mother we were going into Walter's woods to look for one thing or another. I had that feeling again. That sick feeling in the pit of my stomach, that let me know either something was very wrong, or I was about to get into big trouble. I just ignored it, as hard as it was, trying my best not to puke violently.

I waited patiently for Minny outside the house, as she told our little white lie. We didn't even think of the fact that the show was about 2 hours long, and we would have to explain where we were for all that time.

I seemed to forget about time a lot back then. I remember mother would always say to us you had better be home before dark but I usually never made it home before the night's sky fell. I am imagining it was because I was grounded most of the time. When I did actually get to go out and up the road (as we called it with the other kids) I would completely forget.

I would forget until I would look up and see the stars in the night sky then my heart would once again go to my throat knowing I had forgotten to keep track of the sun going down. We also had no watches or clocks as no one could afford something that expensive to wear on their arm. Time was so unimportant as a kid until you were grounded, then it went on forever or seemed to stop altogether.

We were just so convinced we would never be caught. The excitement, well, that was just too much to bear. We would have no way to explain our absence, but we were beyond the point of no return.

My Own Clairvoyance

We made it past the old post office, right across the road to be exact. I saw it coming in my mind's eye, just like Granny Linster, before it even happened. I knew and foresaw exactly what was going to happen. Exactly like a rerun of an old movie. I just stood there in shock, unable to move a muscle, frozen in time and space. It was as if the world stood still for a minute while all time stopped, and then went into slow motion.

There she came, old Mrs. Hobbs out of the taxi. I swear it was the devil himself that day that took over her shadow. At least that's what I saw in my mind's eye. I saw the horns protruding from the head in her shadow on the sidewalk. It wasn't just my overactive imagination. The knife she wielded appeared out of nowhere, or so it seemed. It looked to me like it was about 6 feet long, even though later reports said it was only a butcher's knife.

She ran toward the phone booth as I stood there paralyzed in fear, knowing exactly what was going to happen next. My cousin Minny had been walking for a while before she realized that I was no longer with her.

Some poor woman standing in the phone booth, getting ready to call her husband, having no idea what was going on. Minnie stopped, and to her horror, Mrs. Hobbs started swinging her butcher knife. I clearly remember the knife swinging through the air. The 9 month old baby she had been carrying in her arms fell like a bag of groceries to the ground. I really can't even remember if he cried.

I don't think the woman in the phone booth ever even knew what had happened. She was dead before she even hit the ground. I don't think in all of my life, I have ever felt more sorrow for another human being than I did that day. That 50 cents I had swindled out of my grandfather suddenly felt like two 10 pound weights in my pocket. The shame I felt for my actions that day burned a hole right though my heart. Once people realized what was happening, a couple of them tried to pull the crazy and murderous Mrs. Hobbs off the innocent woman. By then it was too late.

There was such a commotion. Unfortunately Minny and I were stuck in the crowd, unable to pass the police line. Someone had apparently called my Granny Milly and my mother, and told them that they had seen us up at the doctor's office which was right next to the old post office where the terrible act of the young woman's murder had taken place. My Granny Milly was so scared. I had never seen her that afraid. She thought for sure something terrible had happened to one of us. The 2 of them came tearing up the road to get us. Man, were we in big trouble! My one consolation was that Minny didn't get a beating like I did. After all, I did talk her into it, and I felt really bad for it.

We later found out that old Mrs. Hobbs had thought that this young lady she killed in cold blood was having an affair with her husband, Harry Hobbs. I don't remember the young woman's name, but I do remember she was only 22 years old. Her poor baby boy was left in this cruel world without a mother to love him. I knew exactly how he felt.

The whole town was in quite a state of shock for a while after that. Old Mrs. Hobbs went willingly with the cops. There wasn't much security in the 'old butter scotch palace' or the 'nut house' as we called it. I think it was only natural that people were afraid she might escape, and try to claim another victim.

Unsolved Mystery

There was a whole other scandal from years back. It happened a few years after I was born but I was too young to really remember much of it, just brief flashes of memory here and there whenever someone brought it up. Most of it was a lot of rumors and speculation, but once this poor young girl was murdered, the whole town was convinced of what happened so many years before.

Back then, there was another "Mrs. Hobbs." I don't even know what her name was I believe it was Jane. She was only referred to as the *"1st Mrs. Hobbs."* I do remember how everyone talked about how nice she was after she disappeared, but then again, in this town you were a "dirty rotten scoundrel" until the day you died.

Then, automatically and suddenly you became that "poor man" or that "poor woman." It was kind of messed up. I mean, after all, it is either you like someone or you don't.

Why pretend?

According to the story, this woman Jane, I'm not sure what her last name was before she got married but she married into the Hobbs family. She married a guy named John who was a police officer. Jane's sister Diane lived with them for quite a while from what I understand. Then one fateful night in March, 1976 Jane Hobbs disappeared never to be seen or heard from again. I guess no one will ever really know the truth except the people involved.

Jane had always suspected that her husband John and her sister Diane were having an affair although she was never able to prove it. Being a creature of habit, Jane would go out to a poker game every Friday night and never missed a game.

This one particular night however, for whatever reason Jane decided to leave the poker game early and head home, maybe it was the storm outside or maybe it was her guts telling her it was time to face the truth about her philandering husband and her covetous sister.

She arrived home and caught her husband and her sister right in the act of making love. Jane naturally became enraged and a huge fight ensued with Jane first attacking her sister. That is apparently when her husband John grabbed a hold of Jane. It seemed that both of them (Jane's sister and John) beat her to death with a hockey stick in the kitchen of Jane's own home.

Once Jane was dead, they had to cover up the crime somehow. So, they proceeded to murder the dog and smear his blood all over the kitchen floor to cover up Jane's blood. Remember, back then there was no DNA evidence to prove that she had been murdered. It was just remnants of dried blood for the police investigation after they had cleaned up the bloody mess from the murder of Jane and her hapless dog.

Rumor had it that John's best friend just happened to be the dog catcher, Louie. He also owned a contracting business which consisted of selling large excavation machinery such as back hoes, tractors, etc. He had the contract at the time to put an extension on the Sea view Manor to make it larger. The Sea view Manor was the only retirement home in the town of Glace Bay and still is to this day I believe. The night of Jane's disappearance, interestingly, Louie was seen by many witnesses (as people are very nosey in small towns) out there at 2 AM digging up the Sea view Manor's foundation. People logically speculated that he was actually helping John bury Jane's body. After all, why else would someone be out digging up a foundation at 2 AM?

A further rumor was that Louie took Jane's body and threw her in the lye pit to dissolve her bones so that no actual evidence of her murder could ever be found. Louie had the lye pit dug on his property to dispose of all the stray dogs he would catch. Once dissolved in the pit, no one could ever prove that he had taken their dog.

Jane's sister, Diane, admitted to hitting Jane but not actually murdering her. She was sentenced to 4 years in prison for manslaughter because Jane's body was never found. To this day they are still looking for her remains. Jane's husband, John was never convicted however. The only evidence they could bring against him in the court of law was a bloody hockey stick which apparently was not enough to convict him.

***

CHAPTER 14

Kimmy

When death came calling as it often did in our small town, all adults were afraid to move, probably out of fear of who was going to be called home by the grim reaper next. They gingerly walked around on egg shells thinking, and fearing they could and would be next. I used to find it all quite amusing.

When you are young, you think you are invincible. Nothing can touch you, especially not death. That's exactly how I felt before this next death was to hit our town (and me especially). It felt so good to feel invincible. I loved the fear I created in all of my so-called friends. I loved the power, even at such a young age, it was intoxicating. I look back now, and realize it was because I really had no power over my own life at home (as with most bullies who are themselves from bullying households).

Death to me up until this point was just something that I and every one of my friends assumed happened to "old" people. Our definition of old people, was anyone over the age of
30!

A Prisoner Buried in a Tomb

I was never really afraid, even with the dreams. Those crazy dreams. I am not sure if it was death I was dreaming about, or if it was imprisonment. Still to this day I remember so clearly how the dream went. I had the same dream often. It was my brother Joe and I, always in this dream. We were on trial for stealing something, mostly food I think. What I remember most in this dream was the palpable fear. I knew what the crowd was going to do, even though I had never seen anything remotely like it in real life.

The judge was always my mother, or I should say, I knew it was my mother. Even though she was in a man's body, I still knew it was her. She would sentence us for our crime (s), and
the whole town would march us down this long road to the town church. Surrounding the church were concrete tombs. Some of them were built right off the side of the old stone structure. Some of them were scattered all over the grounds. They would take Joe and me, and force us into those tombs, and close the concrete slab over us, sealing us to our fate forever. The most terrifying part of this dream was when they pushed the concrete slab over the top of us, and we were left alone in complete darkness. Sometimes after I had these dreams, I would be haunted for days by them. I was so completely terrified that I couldn't sleep in my bed in a dark room.

Sometimes dreams have meanings. I believe it is up to us to figure out what they are trying to tell us. I believe the dreams I used to have of Joe and I being imprisoned was my mind trying to figure out what was going on. For most of my childhood, it felt like I was a prisoner. Until the minute I escaped my childhood home and the hell I was in living there, I was in a tomb with no hope of escape.

The best dreams I had however, would be the dreams I would have of flying. They were the best dreams of all. The freedom I felt in those dreams was the freedom I had been spending my life searching for.

Then, there was a new dream. This dream I started to have over the next couple of weeks was one of the scariest ones I ever had, but no matter how hard I thought about it, I could not figure it out what it meant. It became so bad; I didn't want to go to sleep. It was terrifying. I would be on the pond skating, and I remember it was bitter cold (when wasn't it!). I kept skating around in circles. It was anything but fun, but I couldn't stop myself from going around in those circles. My legs were sore, and my lungs were freezing. It was getting harder and harder to breathe. Suddenly the ice started to crack. I could hear it. The sound was almost deafening. I just kept skating closer and closer to the crack. I felt as if I had no control over my body. I started sliding out of control. I watched in horror as the crack in the ice got bigger and bigger.

I was in a state of panic, frantically grabbing at the ice, trying desperately to hold on, but I knew it was pointless. Just as I hit the freezing water, I'd wake up, drenched with sweat, and being freezing cold. I couldn't understand the dream. Spring was coming, and I knew there
was no way I would ever think about going out onto the ice, especially to go skating. What I didn't realize was that it was not me in the dream. I was actually dreaming of something that had not yet happened to someone very close to me.

Disappointment

My mother told us our father was coming to get us that day for a Sunday visit, our real father that is. We didn't know him very well because we didn't see him that often. He was supposed to take us every Sunday after church for the rest of the day. Most of the time, he would never show up. According to my mother and step-father, dad was a drunk and that's why he was always so unreliable, and constantly making promises he could not keep. Almost like clockwork, he would call every Sunday right after we got home from church, and tell my mother he was coming to get us after we had our usual Sunday dinner. We would all get so excited, rushing up the stairs to get ready, after forcing our food down. Not that the Sunday dinner was tasty, it never was.

We were afraid if we didn't get outside, he would drive by, think we weren't waiting for him, and just keep on going back home. He was always so good to us. It was like a whole different world at his place. I cannot I remember him yelling at us, or giving us a good beating, like Mother did.

He made sure we knew that he loved us. When we did go for a visit, I used to think maybe he was drunk. We kids were completely out of control, and yet he still put up with us.

So many times, though we would all go outside and wait for him on the old, homemade garbage box, but he wouldn't show up. We would sit there for hours hoping and waiting. About every half hour or so, one of us would go running into the house to check the time. This was one of my biggest disappointments in my life. Even worse than all of the punishments my mother had rained down on me.

Finally, after about 3or 4 hours, my mother would yell out to us to come in. This was the part I hated most. She would always say, *"See, I told you that no good son of a bitch wasn't going to come."*

I remember trying to fight back the tears as I listened to her go on and on about how
bad my father was. I hated her more at those times, than I ever did in my entire short life.

What I did find out in later years from my father, who would not lie, was that every week my mother would call him the minute we got outside, and tell him that she changed her mind. We were not allowed to go to visit him on that particular day. Do you think she would tell us kids that he wasn't coming? No, she enjoyed thinking of us sitting out there in our misery, with our
hearts breaking. This Sunday, we all went out to wait on the old garbage box as usual, hoping with all of our hearts that we would not be disappointed. We sat there with nothing to say, just waiting and half expecting my father to supposedly cancel again.

It was always a nice surprise when he showed up right on time at 1:30PM. My father always liked to take us to see his sisters and brothers, whenever we went to visit him. I just loved it. There were always all kinds

122

of cookies and treats that were actually bought from the store, something we never got at home. These were some of the very few happy childhood memories I had to hold onto through a lot of rough times.

A Vision of What's to Come

All was well up until it was time to go home. Suddenly my stomach started to knot up in fear. I stood there feeling like I was going to be so sick. I lost all the color in my face, and I thought for sure I was going to faint. My father asked me what was going on, but I couldn't give him an answer. I had no idea what was going on myself, or what was wrong with me The drive home seemed to take forever. I usually wished the drive would never end. I had that surreal feeling again, like everything was happening in slow motion. I knew something very bad was about to happen. I just wasn't sure what it was.

I could see the fire truck and ambulance long before they appeared on the road. My father had to pull over to let them pass. I could feel my anxiety growing. I knew she was dead, one of my best friends, Kimmy. No one even had to tell me. I could feel her spirit riding with me in the back of my father's old beat up car.

"I wonder what's going on" my father said almost to himself.

"Kimmy is dead." I said to him almost in a whisper.

"We're telling," my sister and two brothers said in unison.

"You're wishing death on someone, you're gonna get it!"

Kimmy was a part of our gang. She wasn't born in our small town like I was. She was a transplant from New Waterford. There were very few of us who weren't born there so we had to stick together. She had so many brothers and sisters that you really couldn't keep track of them. There was of course a lot of talk about the family and the number of kids they had when they moved into their half of Company House on Center Avenue. The question that seemed to be on everyone's mind was where they were keeping all of those kids it was after all just 3 small bedrooms in the house. Kimmy was as brave as I was me and pretty tough as well. Not too many kids messed with her and if she couldn't beat you down she had older sisters that would do it for her. That's just the way it was, survival of the fittest started for most of us kids, even at such a young age.

My father lectured the 3 kids about telling on each other until we came upon the scene of an accident. The look on my father's face told me he knew it was something serious. The Mounties (Royal Canadian Mounted Police) were there, so he knew that someone must have died. He stopped the car to see if he could find out what was happening. He got out of the car and began to ask people in the gathering crowd if they knew who had been hurt, or what was going on. I remember clearly the blood on the snow shining bright red under the street lights. I looked up at the sky watching the falling snow and I knew in my heart of hearts that Kimmy was gone . All anyone had was a lot of questions, and no real answers. They could only tell us someone had been hit by a car, and there were some witnesses the Mounties were talking to.

When we arrived home, the phone was ringing off the wall. As per usual, all of us kids were told to go straight to bed. Thankfully, or so I thought, I was off the hook. That was not to be the case. My brother, Vin started as soon as he got the chance. Telling my mother about how I had said Kimmy was dead. I was halfway up the stairs, hoping that she was so busy on the phone that she wouldn't hear him. She did. It seemed like whenever it had to do with me, she never missed a beat and beat down.

She called me downstairs after she had finished talking to Vin, to ask me what horrible thing I had done this time. I knew there was no point in denying it, so I just came right out and told her that Kimmy was dead.

"How do you know that!?" she screamed at me, with her eyes bugging out of her head like she was possessed. I had no answer. I remember being so afraid. Afraid of what the consequences were for me being so blunt.

"I just know." I told her.

I used to think I was always prepared for her rages, but who was I kidding.

"You are such a filthy liar," she screamed at me, her fists pounding on my head and back as I tried to protect myself.

"How could you make up such a terrible lie?" she continued. She was frothing at the mouth, or at least she was in my mind.

"You know what happens to evil people like you," she yelled in between gasps of breath.

"When you wish death on someone. You will rot in hell."

Those were the last words I remember before I blacked out. When I came to, I was on the floor, blood pouring from my nose, and my mother screaming, *"You are grounded!"* I didn't even bother to ask how long or for what. I was always grounded after a good beating. I went to bed crying that night like I did so many others, but this time I was praying that I was wrong. God only knows, I thought, what would happen to me if what I had said was right. So I prayed almost until the crack of dawn, but once again God wasn't listening. I guess he was busy elsewhere.

I didn't have to wait long. My mother came in at 6 AM screaming like a raving lunatic. At least it was better than ice cold water, I remember thinking to myself.

"You made her die! You wished it on her."

Those were the only coherent words I could make out. That's how I found out what I had felt and foresaw about Kimmy was true. I wished at that moment in time I could just curl up into a ball and disappear. It would be better than facing the stares and ridicule I knew were to come because I had opened my big mouth. The whole house was in an uproar by this point.

Kimmy really was dead. It certainly proved that I was evil. Otherwise how would I have known she died?

Once again, I received another good beating. The dream I was having, I found out later, was actually a dream about Kimmy... a dream of the horrible way that she had died. She had been sledding with another friend of ours on a hill by the Co-Op. Cliff, he was the town drunk, was driving up the road when he lost control of his car. He drove right up the hill Kimmy was on, just as she was sliding down on her magic carpet sled. He drove over her. Cliff was so drunk, he had no idea he hit anything, let alone a small girl like Kimmy.

Poor Kimmy! My heart ached for her. She had been caught under the car according to witnesses, but she had still been alive. She had been, as I had heard, trying desperately to find a way out from under the car. Cliff never realized what was going on, and drove another 200 feet up the road, before losing control again. He drove right into the pond at the end of the Co-Op hill. The weight of the car had been too much, and the ice broke, carrying Kimmy to her watery grave. I could see Kimmy in my mind's eye, realizing this was to be the end of her all too short life. It tore me apart inside, especially at her funeral.

Of course, mother had told everyone my prediction about Kimmy's death and how I had wished it on her. Kimmy and I had had a fight a few days before and were still on the mend with our friendship when her death took place. While at the funeral it seemed as though everyone one in our town was there. The whole school and every prying eye was upon me as I walked up to the casket to say my final goodbyes. I wished and cursed God at that time for it not being me in that casket. Why did I have to suffer so much at the hands of a mad woman when there was a real grieving mother and family that would miss their daughter so very much? People looked at me a lot differently from that day forward, fear mostly because they began to realize I had been given the second sight same as my Granny Linster.

Cliff somehow managed to free himself, and took off running. Sometimes I think maybe he knew what he had done. It took the Mounties a couple of week to track him down. I was devastated. I thought that being young made me invincible. I was so sure I didn't have to worry about dying for quite a long time. I started to become very curious about death and dying after that. It became almost like an obsession. I still carry that with me to this day. That, and memories of Kimmy.

***

CHAPTER 15

How I wish I Could Die

"Can things get any worse?" I sat there thinking to myself. I was still grounded for supposedly causing Kimmy's death. It was so cold outside, but I sat there anyway, not caring if I froze to death. It was still better than being in the house with that monster I called my mother. I started to think about freedom once again.

The one thing I really didn't mind about being grounded was that I could sit and dream and for a while, I could forget about all of my troubles. I think that was my only means of escape so many times. When I think about it today, that was the first time I ever became depressed. I was depressed and desperate. I needed to be away from this horrible place I called home. That's when I started to think of my newest plan.

My mother and stepfather had finally broken me. I really felt like I could no longer live this horrible life. I wanted to be dead, like Kimmy. Not in the horrible, painful way that she did, but I definitely wanted to die. I mean, what was the point? Was I only put on this earth to suffer at the hands of a mad woman? I was, in my opinion and everyone else's from what I heard, just a useless rotten kid. Hell, I couldn't even get my own mother to love me.

How could I go on? In my child's mind at the time, this was the best and only way out. My newest and greatest plan. There was no other way to get the freedom I so desperately wanted short of killing myself which I thought of often but then I would never make it to heaven (if there was one). I would be stuck in purgatory for a 1000 years according to our church. I was almost giddy thinking about it. No more beatings, no more groundings, no more of anything... just freedom.

When I was grounded, I tended to think way too much. I would be grounded for what seemed like forever, and then I would get bored. I sat there and thought of a lot of stupid things to do to get myself into more trouble. This time was just like any other grounding.

I was in trouble for one thing, and before you knew it, I was given a couple of more weeks for some other stupid thing I had done.

Dirty Water

It was Sunday, bath day. Every Sunday, all of us kids had to take our weekly bath. It was pretty gross when I think about it today. We always went from oldest to youngest. Vin, being the oldest always got the clean water, then it was my turn and so on.

We were never to replace the water. That would cost too much money. We weren't even allowed to add any hot water, so when I would get in, the water was usually ice cold. I would turn the tap just the slightest little bit so no one could hear it running downstairs, hoping that it would warm up even 1 degree. Sometimes I swore that Vin would stay in there just to torment me by letting me get a nice cold bath. We were supposed to be brother and sister, but we were more like mortal enemies most days! It really didn't matter how dirty any of us were. We still had to use the same water. If it was a good day of playing outside, the only one who ever really got clean was Vin.

Whenever my sister got her turn in the tub, it was my job to wash her hair, and make sure she was "clean" (even in the filthy water). We usually ended up messing around so much that neither her, nor her hair ever got close to being clean.

Tonight, I had come up with a plan, or a practical joke was more like it. Me and my stupid plans! I told Ann I would wash her hair, and then she had to lay in the tub as if she was dead. I told her to pretend she had drowned. I think I was just so completely fascinated with death since

129

Kimmy had died. I can't believe how stupid we were (or should I say I was). My sister though, was just as dumb as I was since she had agreed to it. I told her after I had finished washing her hair to make a loud bang, just like she had fallen and she did, of course. It really wasn't as loud as we thought it was, because no one heard it downstairs (or cared).

I ran down the stairs anyway, yelling that Ann had fallen in the bath tub, and banged her

head. I told my mother I thought she might be drowning. I imagine I must have been very convincing as I don't think I had ever seen my mother move so fast. She went tearing up the stairs. By then it was too late for me to change my story. I knew I was in big trouble. Ann realized the trouble we were going to get into, so she had jumped out of the tub and began to

dry herself off like she had no idea what was going on. I wanted to kill her at that very moment. I wished I had really tried to drown her!

Needless to say, I went to bed with a real good beating, and no supper. I think that's when I realized how hopeless my situation really was. I thought no one would ever

know how much I hurt inside. So I decided to end it all.

Time to Die

I didn't even take the usual 6 months or so to think to myself if I really wanted to go through with my plan. I knew that this was the night, no matter what. I waited up until I was sure everyone was sleeping. As quietly as I could, I snuck into the bathroom. I opened the medicine cabinet and proceeded to swallow as many pills as I could. I had no idea what any of them were. I just knew I had to end this misery that I was destined to be in.

I started to feel sick, not from the pills, but from the massive amounts of water I had to drink to get them down. I definitely wasn't used to taking pills. I was holding back the vomit, and decided I must have taken enough to die. I made my way back to my bed in the dark, and laid down, waiting to die, and to be released from this hell I called life.

I must have fallen asleep, laying there wondering what it would feel like in Hell. The next thing I knew, I woke up and it was morning. I don't think I had ever been so disappointed in my entire short life! I lay there and cried, until I knew my mother was on her way up the stairs with the icy water. Now I was really afraid. I knew my punishment would be severe for this stunt I had pulled. Not only did I not die like I had planned, but most of my mother and stepfather's medicines were gone.

The whole time I was laying there waiting to die, all I could think of was how bad my mother was going to feel for the things she had done to me. Now, all I could think was how bad I was going to feel after she was done with me. To my surprise, nothing was ever mentioned. For months after taking the pills, I wondered why God hated me so. Why would he not let me die? But I had no answers. I guess my time wasn't up. It was not time to let me die.

***

CHAPTER 16

Womanhood

The summer was finally coming, and surprisingly enough, it had been a few weeks since I had gotten myself into any kind of trouble! Things were definitely looking up! I was still the holy terror of the town, but thankfully I no longer felt like ending my life. There was something about the smell of the air at that time of year that made me feel alive. I was thinking to myself that if I had to be stuck here, I might as well do what I did the best. I was going to cause as many people as much misery as I could!

That is exactly what I did. I still craved that freedom, and I knew if I waited long enough I would eventually get it. After all, good things come to those who wait. Finally school was out, and it was grading day. I had all but forgotten the whole saying about how death comes in 3's. I had other things to worry about.

I was becoming a woman, according to a conversation I overheard between my mother and Granny Milly. I was only 10 years old at the time. I had no idea what they were talking about, but it sounded important enough to me. So important, in fact, that I didn't even hear Vin sneak up behind me, and catch me listening. Of course he told on me, but my mother could not do anything for fear of Granny Milly. *"Children should be seen and not heard"* was the expression used by all of the adults. I knew I would get it later, but I didn't care. I wanted to know what becoming a woman was all about.

My mother got me a training bra from one of my cousins, so I assumed that meant I was now a woman, and that was the end of it. Boy was

I wrong! That was only the beginning. I was so embarrassed and uncomfortable in this thing that was supposed to be perfectly natural and joyous. I was the only girl in grade 5 who had to wear this ridiculous thing! I almost didn't even bother to wear it. I knew I had to though, or face my mother's wrath.

I tried so hard to hide it, but the boys noticed it right away. They teased me cruelly and relentlessly. It just made my fury grow, and hate that little town, and the people in it that much more. To make matters worse, I was growing hair all over my body in places I had no idea hair could or should grow. It was so gross and frightening to me at the time. I knew very little of what was happening to me, only that I was going through puberty (whether I liked it or not). Things would have been a lot easier if I had someone there to explain everything to me.

<u>A Difficult Coming of Age</u>

To my mother, I think it was a big shame, something we could never talk about. We had a few sex education classes at school, and they gave us a book. My mother gave me a half hour to read it, then it was simply thrown into the coal stove. It was, after all, in her eyes, a dirty book. It was so hard to be interested, when everyone in the class was laughing and joking like they already knew all about it. The truth was that, none of us had a clue. I would not dare let anyone in that class know that I was curious about the changes we would all go through, as if because I was first I held some great key to the mystery of puberty.

I had to keep up an image. It all seemed to happen so quickly, I felt like I was stuck between two worlds. One was being a woman, and having all the boys' attention because you had boobs. The other was being a child, still playing with dolls and not being ashamed of it. It was a terrible and confusing time for me. I remember we were all going to the beach when I first became aware of just how embarrassing these changes to my body were becoming. I was kneeling in the back seat, looking out the window, when my brother Vin looked over at me and saw the long hairs protruding from my under arms.

"That's disgusting!" he told my mother. *"She needs to shave."*

I was so embarrassed but curious at the same time. *"You mean I could actually shave this off?"* I thought to myself.

My dreams of a normal life were short-lived when I heard my mother's short reply.

"No" she told Vin, *"She will not shave." I have never shaved under my arms or my legs in my entire life and neither will she."*

That was that, or so she thought. I would not give up that easily. Up until this point, I really wasn't aware of how long the hair under my arms or on my legs got. When I did have that moment of clarity, I became the most shy and awkward person you could ever meet. I was told by my friends that it was all a part of becoming a woman. That, however, did not make me feel any better. I thought I could not feel any less normal when the absolutely worst thing in the world had happened to me.

I got the 'dreaded curse', a.k.a. my period. I thought it was just one more way for God to punish me for being born evil. I was scared to death to tell my mother. What would she say? We never had the kind of mother-daughter relationship where we could actually talk about things like this.

Red and White Pants

I was having flashbacks of a girl in my class when she got her period. She was a Jehovah's Witness, and never quite fit in with most of the class mainly because of her religion. We just rejected her for being different. She wore white pants that particular day, and when she raised her hand to go to the bathroom, no one thought anything of it. That is, until she stood up. The whole class seemed to see it at once, a giant red stain right on the back of her pants.

134

We all began to snicker, but not once did it ever occur to any of us girls to let her know. I think it was just too uncomfortable a situation to be brought up, especially at our age. When she came back from the bathroom, she sat down as if nothing had happened. Maybe she didn't notice, or maybe she was just too ashamed of what was happening to her body, but either way, it made life a lot harder for her for a long time after that. There were so many rumors from the girls that because of her religion she was not allowed to wear maxi pads. I laugh thinking about it today, but back then it did seem quite possible. I was thinking of poor Betty, and then I knew I was pretty much screwed.

My mother would not let me shave under my arms, or my legs. What would she do in a situation like this? Finally, I decided that there was no way I was going to be humiliated like Betty. I had no choice but to tell my mother. It wasn't as bad as I thought it would be when I told her.

"The curse is not a bad thing." my friends explained later, *"It is just something that is never talked about."* after I came clean with them.

This I could definitely not talk about, I thought to myself. My mother went out and bought me what seemed to be a huge box of maxi pads, or "Kotex" as they were called and known. They were the most awful things I had ever seen, and the most uncomfortable. I wished that day that I had been born a boy, and once a month, every month for a long time, I wished that same thing.

It felt like you had a roll of toilet paper stuck between your legs, and you were trying to walk without anyone noticing. It was awful! It was definitely one of the worst experiences of my life.

So, here it was summer. I had hairy arms, hairy legs, and I was bleeding from the most unnatural place in the world to me. To make matters worse, my mother never took the time to explain to me that when you put a maxi pad on, the sticky side had to go down so it would stick to your

135

underwear. It was a painful experience, to say the least. She must have been checking

up on me, because she took me aside one day, and told me I was doing it wrong. I think that is the only conversation we ever had about me becoming a woman, short and to the point.

As an adaptive behavior, I always made sure I kept my arms down whenever possible, so no one would notice the massive amounts of hair growing there. How could I explain I was not allowed to shave? I never even thought to take a pair of scissors, and at least trim it. One day, I think it was boys that brought me to this point, but I got sick and tired of trying to hide all of my body hair. I knew all of the girls I hung out with were snickering behind my back, but not one of them had the guts to say anything to my face.

Dull Blade

I had another one of my brilliant plans, you could call it. I decided that I was going to shave my underarms, my legs and even my hair if I felt like it. I was so sick of being told what to do yet I was still a chicken at the same time.

I waited until everyone was out. I was so excited about my latest adventure. I can't remember where they went, but at least they were gone. I had picked up one of my step-fathers dull used razors out of the garbage the day before, all so I could be prepared.

This was my very first time shaving. I honestly had no clue what I was doing. I proceeded to run the dull razor up and down my dry legs, thinking it was supposed to burn and be painful. That was until I noticed blood, and I knew this was definitely not supposed to happen. I looked down at my leg. There was blood everywhere. I had taken quite

a gash of skin off with the dull razor. I was in a state of panic, not just from the blood, but also from the thought of what my mother was going to do to

136

me when she got home. I knew once she got wind of my latest stunt, my summer and fall would be over.

After I had calmed down somewhat, I tried to stop the bleeding. Once this was accomplished, I sat down to think. I decided after some contemplation, I would tell my mother that I fell running up the stairs. To me at the time, it was the only way I would ever be able to explain the cut I had made from shaving. All I had to do was bruise my already sore and bleeding leg, so she would never guess my deception.

The cut on my leg was throbbing, but I had to do it to save myself from the beating I knew was coming. I got the hammer, and hit my shin with as much force as I could take to make a bruise right where the cut was. It was so painful, but then I knew she would at least believe me, or so I hoped. My mother didn't even notice. I actually had to bring it to her attention. I limped around for about a week after that, in lots of pain, but it was better than facing my mother's wrath. Becoming a woman really sucked.

***

CHAPTER 17

Old Hag Syndrome

I woke up in a sweat, soaked to the bone (again). That thing was happening to me again. That thing I could never dare breathe a word about to anyone. I knew they would surely think I had lost my mind, and take me to the old *"Butter Scotch Palace"* once again. This time, they would leave me there for good. I always knew when "it" was about to happen, yet I was completely powerless to stop it.

<u>Strong Winds Bring Tortured Souls</u>

I went to bed at night, I would look out my window from the top bunk, staring and wishing it was just my imagination, or the sound of the wind blowing. It may sound strange to some, but I could always tell by the way the trees were blowing, feeling the wet mist in the air, and on my skin, that it was going to happen. When this strange phenomena would happen to me, the wind was always howling through the trees in a certain way, and it scared me to no end.

My Granny Linster used to say the wind was carrying the spirits to the other side when it blew like that through the trees. In my mind's eye I could almost see the spirit of the wind or maybe it was the spirits in the wind that were reaching out grabbing at anything to keep them from leaving. When this happened, a light mist formed on your skin that sent chills up and down your spine. The streets seemed to empty of all people and living creatures, everyone locked in their house for the evening hoping their soul wouldn't be the one being taken .

I don't know about anyone else, but the hair on the back of my neck would stand straight on end. This was supposed to be the spirits saying goodbye to this world, and moving onto the next. Some of the spirits, my Granny Linster would say, were not too happy to be going so soon from this plane of existence. That's when the strange things would start to happen to me (and probably a lot of other people).

My Granny Linster told all us kids strange stories of the souls who refused to go into the wind. They were very unhappy in this life, but even sadder now that their time here was up. Those unhappy souls, she would say pointing her boney finger at us, were no good. They had caused a lot of trouble here in this life. They knew, of course, that they weren't going to heaven. The wind was going to carry them straight to the pits of Hell, she would say, her voice rising as she spoke. Those poor tormented souls, as she would call them, would do anything not to go there.

She would tell us of how when the wind was carrying them to their destiny, they would
howl, and try to grab anything along the way to try to hang onto this plane. Mostly, what they would try to grab, were small kids and animals. These were apparently the easiest to grab, from their point of view.

"They especially love", she said, *"the kids with sickness inside of them, or worse yet, the ones that were evil. Those ones that already had a mark on their soul."*

My granny would warn us on nights like this, to be sure to sleep on our sides, and to keep a pillow securely up against our stomachs. The stomach, she always told us, was the center of your being. That was the only way they could get at your soul. I would listen to these stories, terrified, because I was so sure that was exactly what was happening to me. They were trying
to steal my soul because of the mark of the devil I had on my soul.

"When the moon is at its fullest", my Granny Linster would say, *"lay on your side and put a pillow as tight as you can up against your stomach."*

This position presented quite a problem for me though because we only had one very thin pillow each. Combine that with a 4 by 8 sheet of plywood, with a very thin mattress on top. The

mattress was so thin, there weren't even any springs in it, and just a piece of foam was all it really was. It was covered in old flowered material to be disguised as a mattress. It was so worn in the middle; it was just like sleeping on the plywood itself. That would make for a very sore neck for days afterwards, if I was to give up the pillow for my neck to cover my stomach.

An even greater problem was that on most nights it was much too cold to take the 2 thin blankets I owned, and try to scrunch them to my stomach. So each night when I would see the trees blowing that certain way, and I could hear the cries of the souls being carried away by the winds, I had a decision to make. I could spend the night freezing, clutching the thin blankets to my stomach, or I could lay under the blankets covered from head to toe, and try to stay awake, hoping the spirits would pass by without noticing me.

Walk-Ins

"Walk-ins", is what my Granny Linster called them. Oh, they were clever, she would say, preying on people that no one would ever really notice were different. The spirits would come in the middle of the night to those unsuspecting kids, pull their souls right out of their bodies, and then jump right in. No one would ever know.

One day, I even dared to ask what happened to the soul of the kid. *"Well"*, she said, *"Looking at me with her small beady eyes, your soul just floats for a while."*

140

"You see", she said, *"you are still in a way attached to your body by this long thin silver thread. It doesn't last long,"* she said with a sigh, *"those who steal the bodies usually aren't stupid. They seem to figure out a way to get rid of that thread."*

I wanted to ask more, but dared not. I knew my mother was listening, and I would get it when I got home. I knew what she said was true. I had fought for my soul against these tortured spirits more than once. It still happens to me, sometimes even now (and no, I am not crazy). Though, with experience I have learned some techniques to ward off these wandering spirits.

As previously mentioned, I always knew when it was going to happen. This night was no different from the rest, or so I thought. I looked out the window on this night, and for some reason it sent a shiver, from the top of my head straight through to the tips of my toes. The knot in my stomach was immediate and sickening, almost making me throw up on the spot. I was in for the fight of my life that night, against some unseen force, and didn't even know it yet.

This day had started out normally enough. My gang and I did all of the things we usually did, but weren't supposed to. I was still very peeved at that old coot, Andrew Read. He was responsible for the loss of my dog Star, as far as I was concerned. Every chance I got, I would go up to the old bastard's farm, and do whatever I could to make his life as miserable as he had made mine.

I would do crazy things, like break his windows by throwing big rocks with notes tied to them, just like I had seen in the movies. The notes were very childish when I think back now, but I was enjoying myself all the same. Sometimes I would commit the most unthinkable crime in our community. I would destroy a portion of his crop. Something like that could get you killed in our town. That was how most people fed their families for the year. Did I care though? No, I didn't. I wanted to hurt him the way that he had hurt me. We were always careful, or so I thought, never to get caught.

We always made sure never to go near the old farm if his truck was anywhere near the house or field. Not careful enough, as it turned out. Old Andrew was finally starting to figure out it was us kids, or maybe he knew all along, and was waiting for his opportunity at retaliation. The first thing he did was buy a salt gun. Being hit by a salt gun is like a 1000 pellets from a BB gun hitting you in one spot at the same time. Then he began to go to the mall every day, which was not like him. In his mind, this was the wife's job, but he was planning. He began to tell everyone in town that he had bought a salt gun, and was not afraid to use it if he caught anyone near his land. He did not, however, spill the beans as to the reason why he was telling people this. For the few who dared ask him, all they got for an answer was a grunt as he walked away.

"Screw him," I said to my gang.

"He's probably full of crap. Salt guns are totally illegal and almost impossible to get."

Some of my gang was scared, although they wouldn't admit it. They just seemed to have an excuse every time I mentioned going up to his farm. There were only a few rebels like me, driven by the excitement of tormenting the old man. I was so sure there was no salt gun. I got braver and braver just to torment the old coot. I was so wrong, boy, was I wrong!

One day when we were least expecting it, he pounced on us like a fox after a rabbit. I say it like that because to me, that is exactly what we were, scared rabbits running in all different directions. Andrew took his truck, parked it down at the shore, and then made his way back to his farm.

I think by this point, we had driven him mad in a way. He was as determined to get us kids, as we were to get him. He hid in the tall grass by the chicken coop, and waited patiently. It wasn't too long before we fell into his trap. That old coot waited until we were almost right on top of him before he jumped out at us. I have to admit, I was scared. I could see the madness in his eyes. I don't think I have ever seen anyone that angry before, except my mother of course and I wasn't even sure then.

He cocked his salt gun, the one I was sure he didn't have, and started shooting aimlessly. He didn't care who he shot, or where he shot you. I think I was the first one to get it, taking one right in the arse. I couldn't sit for over a week without the most awful pain. I thought it would never heal.

In our panic and shock, it took us a minute to realize what was going on, but when we did, it was like something out of a movie. There he was the old coot Andrew, screaming at us like a crazed lunatic, shooting at everything and nothing, even sometimes in midair. All of us kids were scrambling in different directions at the same time. It was as if time had stopped. We seemed to be running in circles, bumping into each other over and over again.

Finally, someone started for the woods. We all followed with Andrew hot on our trail. Thankfully, he was way too old to run very far, so we made our escape, or so we thought. I was still running like my life depended on it for the shore when I heard Sherry, one of my friends, screaming. It was not a normal kind of scream, and I knew something was wrong. I was trying to figure what direction it was coming from when someone grabbed me by the arm. I spun so quickly, thinking it was Andrew that I lost my balance and fell right into Tammy, another friend of mine. She was yelling that Sherry had fallen into a hole of an old strip mine. Tammy was panicking and it was hard to understand her, but eventually, after I slapped her in the face, she calmed down enough to tell me the old mine was filled with water and Sherry was drowning.

We ran toward the screams, tying our jackets together as we went. Sherry's head was just about to go under again when we reached her. We were able to tie all of our jacket sleeves together to create a kind of makeshift rope, and quickly threw it in to pull her out. We thought for sure this was her end, but thankfully she grabbed on and we were able to pull her to safety.

She was barely out when we heard the familiar sound of the shotgun being cocked again. That old coot Andrew was right on our tail again. There was a feeling of panic in the air as I yelled at everyone to stick together. There was no way I was going to go home with anyone's death on my hands that or any other day.

We all started running as fast as our little legs could carry us. Where we were going, I had no idea. I just knew that we were in big trouble if Andrew was to get a hold of one of us. I am not even sure how most of us missed it, crossing the ditch but we did. Tammy didn't. She was the last one to cross. I guess being the smallest also made her the slowest of us. She ran right through a wasp's nest that was lying, according to her after the fact, right in the middle of the path we had all taken. The wasps, we were told, were the devil's helpers and they were mad!

We tried dragging her away from the angry wasps, but nothing seemed to work. Funny thing is, not one of us got stung as we finally dragged her to the edge of Duggie and Mary's house. We lost Andrew, but now we had an even bigger problem on our hands. We fled towards Duggie's house like the devil was chasing us. Duggie came out looking as scared as we felt.

We didn't have to tell him what was going on. He could see it for himself. He didn't say a word, just got out the hose and started to soak Tammy down.

The ambulance driver told Duggie that if Tammy had been allergic to bees she would have died. I felt so guilty.

Once they left with Tammy in the ambulance, Duggie turned and looked at us with more seriousness than I had ever seen him have.

"You kids," he said, *"woke the nasty spirits, and now there is going to be hell to pay."* I tried to brush him off, but the knot of fear began to grow in my stomach, as he yelled at us for what seemed like forever. I knew in my heart that we had angered Satan's workers, and one of us would have to pay.

Visit From The Old Hag

The moon was full that night, and I could feel the fear as I climbed into my bed. This thing that happened to me always started out the same way. Tonight was different. I knew it was going to happen, so I scrunched all of those thin blankets up to my stomach, and began to pray. I must have fallen asleep when that thing began to happen. I woke up, or should I say my conscious mind woke up. My body however was still asleep, and no matter how hard I tried, I could not move or scream.

It was said that the spirits paralyze your body so it's easier for them to steal your soul. This time when I woke up it was different. I was still on my side with the blankets still scrunched up against my cold body. I could see the demon creature hovering over my body. I had never seen anything like it before, and was never so afraid in my entire life.

The demon thing, beast, or spirit, began to flip me over like I was a rag doll. I was trying to grip the blankets tighter to my stomach, but I knew it was no use. I was completely paralyzed. Before I could fully grasp what was happening to me, the spirit of the beast was sitting on top of my chest, crushing the air slowly out of my lungs.

It had the face of a wolf, with horns protruding from his head instead of ears. He was almost smiling beneath his snarling face. I swear to this day, I could also hear his howls deep within my brain. I was trying desperately to wake myself up, and get out of this nightmare. I saw his hands reach down, with his long gnarled fingers, but could do nothing as he began to pull my

soul from my body. I could feel myself, or my soul, I should say, being pulled, until it was

almost halfway out of my body.

I finally clued in that I had to fight back. It was the fight of my life that night. This beast would pull me out so far, and I would gain a little bit of control, and be able to pull my soul back

in. I tried everything to get myself to wake up, but nothing seemed to be working. Even my screams were only inside my own mind. Finally, when I was almost too exhausted to go on, I remembered what my Granny Linster had told me to do if something like this was ever to happen to me.

"Child", she said, *"almost as if she was speaking to me at that very moment, move your baby finger and break the spell."*

It seemed to take me forever, but I finally was able to begin to move my pinky. Just a bit at first, but I knew I was breaking the spell. The spirit of the beast also began to realize what was happening, and made one final attempt at taking my soul.

In the end, I won, thank God. I would have almost thought I was dreaming the next day, if it wasn't for the large red mark I discovered around my belly button. I never told anyone about that night, but it took me over a week to sleep soundly after that. They still call it the "Old Hag Syndrome" to this day.

***

CHAPTER 18

Dances n' Drugs

I believe that being able to sleep properly really played havoc with me in terms of my thinking and my life in general. Even after I was able to sleep, it still took me forever. I would start to feel myself going into a deep sleep, and then the panic would set in. I would then force myself to wake up.

This caused all kinds of problems for me. After a long night of tossing and turning, I woke up to the usual shock of cold water being thrown in my face. I just lay there and cried.

Thinking, *"Why me God? Why do you hate me so?"* But, there weren't any answers. There just never were. I had wished most days since Kimmy died, that I could die too, but this day was much worse than the others. I think I was overwhelmed with "the curse", as people called it back then.

I just couldn't take it anymore. I needed to get out of this hellhole no matter what the cost. I knew there was no use in trying to kill myself again. I had already tried that, and failed miserably. I did, however, have that itch again for the freedom I so desperately craved. I needed a plan.

The worst part of living in a small town, was that we were so cut off from the rest of the
world. In fact, except for the trip we got to go on to town once every couple of weeks, this town was what most of us kids perceived as our whole world. Most adults also seemed to be in no need to look anywhere outside of our town. Then again they didn't live the silent hell I had been living every day.

Not for me though. I just knew there was something beyond this town. I knew there was a whole other world out there just waiting for me. The one sad fact was, realistically, it was way too hard for me to get to that new world. The closest town was about 12 miles away. To me that might as well have been a million miles. I could not see how I could ever hitchhike there.

Everyone knew each other in our little town. They would pick me up, drive me right back to my mother's house. I had even thought about walking, but I knew that would never happen. The main road that cut us off from the rest of the world was completely dark at night, not even a street light for miles, just woods and more woods. I will admit that as brave as my friends thought I was, I think I would have rather died than walk that road alone at night.

The New Plan

I needed a new plan, and I think I had finally come up with one.

There was a dance every Friday in The Grove. That was another small town about 6 miles away from ours. Anyone who wanted to go to the dance in The Grove had to jump on the bus on Friday night. The bus was free, so all you needed was 2 bucks for the dance and you were as good as in. This sounded simple enough, right? Not for me. It was anything but simple.

There were 2 things stopping me. I didn't have 2 bucks. No one was going to give it to me. Most importantly though, there was no way in hell my mother would ever allow me to go. I think she would have surely killed me just for asking.

I knew in my heart that if I could somehow get to that dance, all of my problems would somehow be solved. I was excited just thinking about it. I knew once I got there, I would be able to hitchhike to the next town without a problem. No one there knew me, so there was no way they could take me home. I could almost taste freedom! It would be pointless to ask my mother if I could go to the dance, but I figured by this point I had nothing to lose. I was always so terrified of asking my mother for anything. I learned from past experiences, that even the smallest things could get me a good beating. A small thing like asking if there was any butter left for my toast in the morning was enough.

I had to ask myself if it would be worth the beating I knew I was going to get. I decided that the answer was definitely yes. If this was going to give me that chance at the freedom I so desperately craved, I would do it, no matter what the consequences. It took me all week to figure out how to bring up the subject. Every time I thought about asking, I would break out in a cold sweat, knowing what the outcome was going to be.

When I Get Older

Finally, I had my new plan. Boy, did it excite me! I would get someone else to ask! I already had someone else in mind, who I knew my mother would have a hard time saying no to, the Heart sisters. They were, I guess you could say, my best friends. They were the only ones who would come and sit with me in the yard on those endless days of grounding. I remember how we would sit on that old swing for hours, talking and dreaming. Dreaming about how one day we were all going to be famous when we grew up. Sometimes that was all that kept me going during those long days. We would talk and talk, always about the same things. About all of the changes we were going to make to our looks, so that we would be beautiful. Jerry, who all of the kids use to call Bubble Arse because of her oversized butt, was going to get jiffy sucked, as we called it. That was the term we used for getting the fat sucked out of her butt. No one would ever make fun of her large rear ever again, and she would, according to all of us, live happily ever after.

149

Terry on the other hand was tall and thin. She was almost 6 feet tall at age 12, a "carpenter's dream", was what all the boys said behind her back. They would snicker as she walked by, saying just loud enough for her to hear and no one else, *"Flat as a board and never been laid, yep, that's Terry."* Her dream was, of course, to grow up and get breast and butt implants.

Then there was me. I was covered in freckles from head to toe I didn't look like the rest of my family and often thought and wished I had been switched at birth and maybe one day my real parents would come waltzing in and rescue me . My brother Vin and his friends would laugh constantly, and say I looked like someone had thrown a bucket of crap at me through a screen door. God, I hated them for that. My dream was to buy this stuff called porcellana, a freckle removal cream. I really believed it would solve all of my problems.

They may not seem like big dreams now, but back then, they were the dreams of changes and better things to come. I didn't have to ask Gerry and Terry twice about talking my mother into letting me go to the dance. I was never so nervous in my whole entire life. I thought I was going to be sick, as I almost changed my mind a million times. The Heart sisters, bless them, would not let me back down, knowing my fear.

They assured me over and over again they would let my mother know I had nothing to do with their asking. I knew they would try, but it was no use. My mother would never believe that.

I pretended to be looking in the cupboard for something while they sat at the table to ask her. I don't think I breathed the whole time, waiting for her to get up and start smacking me. My mother never really cared if our friends were around when she had one of her fits. She started whacking us, and when they left, the real beatings began.

I don't even remember the conversation. All I heard was my mother saying that yes, she thought I could go, as long as the Heart sisters were going to be there. They were given strict instructions to watch me. They weren't sluts or whores, like most of the other girls in our small town, including me.

They pulled it off. I was allowed to go! I couldn't believe it! I thought it was some crazy dream at first, and that I would wake up back in reality any minute. It took every bit of strength and energy I had not to react and show how excited I really was. Now I had to figure out phase 2 of my plan. How was I going to escape once I got there? It seemed easy enough when I thought about it. I would go to the dance like everything was normal.

Once everyone was inside, I would leave. I would tell my friends I was going out for a smoke, and just keep on going until I was out of sight. Then I would hitchhike to the next town, and finally get that freedom I had been searching for my whole life. I wish I thought my plans out a lot better, but I never seemed to be able to.

There were 2 things wrong with this plan. They were very major things I realized once I got there. Firstly, I had never been to this town before. I had no idea which direction I was to go that would bring me to the next town. Secondly, and most important to me, I had never hitchhiked before, and I was scared silly at the prospect. Could I let this opportunity pass me by yet again? I thought not. Finally Friday came, but it seemed to be the longest week of my life.

I wasn't sure if I was more excited about going to the dance, or what I was going to do
once I got there. I was so scared all week, fearing my mother would have a fit and change her mind. She didn't, but it left me exhausted. I got on the bus with the rest of the kids, like I had done it a million times. That old familiar feeling started in the pit of my stomach on the way up the road, and

continued to grow the further away we got from our town. Was this it? Was I finally on my way? I hoped so.

Once I got there, I was a bit, no I should say, very disappointed to see that it was just as dark, if not darker at night than in our small town. God, I hated being such a chicken crap, but I was. Then I decided I would carry out my plan anyway, in spite my fear of the dark woods. I left the dance just as I had intended to, but I didn't get very far.

The darkness was bad enough, but being in a town I didn't know about compounded my fear. In my mind, it also seemed to be getting darker by the minute. That certainly didn't help my cause. I was losing sight of the old fire hall, and was just about to change my mind, when fate stepped in.

Face to face I got with a few of the older guys in my school. *"What's up?"* they said. I thought they were going to keep walking, but they didn't. I wouldn't dare tell them what I was trying to do. I tried to sound as cool as possible. I told them I was just getting out for some fresh air. *"Do you wanna smoke some hash?"* Robert, one of the guys asked. I didn't even hesitate. *"Sure,"* I said, like I had done it a million times. Truthfully I had no idea what hash was, but I played along.

I tried not to show these guys how dumb I really was, so I said before anyone else, *"Let's do it."* I didn't have a clue what we were actually doing. *"We got no papers,"* one of them said.

"No. I got a better idea," Robert said. I was half-scared, half-curious and just plain excited. *"Give me your safety pin,"* he said to me.

He meant the safety pin I wore in my ear as an earring, a sign of coolness back then. I gave it to him without thinking twice. He took it, and skillfully pulled it apart. I was completely transfixed at this point. He then pulled a ballpoint pen from his back pocket, and took it apart. Time seemed to stand still for me as I watched, fascinated. He carefully took a small piece of the hash, stuck it on the end of the pin, and lit it. The hash burned for a

152

few seconds, and then he blew it out. He stuck the hollow pen in his mouth, and began to inhale the smoke.

The smell was not exactly appealing, but I didn't hear anyone else complain, so I just stood there waiting. I couldn't wait to try it. My curiosity had definitely gotten the better of me. All thoughts I had that night of leaving home escaped out the window with my introduction to drugs. I had found something new, and better (for the time being) to escape.

I only had a few puffs of hash that night, but suddenly everything was funny. I could not stop laughing, no matter how hard I tried. We went back to the dance, and all too soon it was time to go home. Finally! I found something else to fill that emptiness inside of me. Drugs! I would go to any end to get more... once I had that first taste.

***

CHAPTER 19

Horseshoes

That's when my quest for a new form of fulfillment began, or maybe a new way to plug a giant hole where the rage had burnt through. It set about such a thirst in my mind and body, that sometimes I thought I would go completely insane. Prior to when I knew what drugs were, I didn't know anyone who used them.

Birds of a Feather

Once I started the descent down that path however, I seemed to draw those types of people to me. It was almost as if I was a magnet. Getting stoned, to me, was the best feeling in the world. I usually got high on my way home every day, and didn't really care if my mother was waiting to beat me. I had found the ultimate feeling. I never realized how easy it was to get those drugs either, but it was. Everyone was willing to share, as long as they weren't getting high alone.

It wasn't hard core drugs like they have today, but back then they were pretty hard core to me. The more I got, the more I wanted. It was like I was a man in the desert dying of thirst, and that was the only thing that (kind of) quenched that thirst. The problem with drugs, like I said before, was that people hated to do them alone, and I was no different. So, like everyone else who does drugs, I had to get everyone else around me to try them too. That wasn't too hard for me most of the time. I could be very persuasive when I wanted to be.

Road To Hell

This was the beginning of the end for me, in more ways than one. My time in this town was almost over. I just didn't know it. I had all but given up but now. I found a new way to fill that hole in the pit of my existence. I knew deep down that it was the devil making me do the drugs. I was so lost at this point, I just couldn't help myself. My biggest regret was opening

that door and letting all of that evil flow in. Once that door was opened, there was no closing it, nor did I want to. I was on top of the world, or so I thought.

Minny, my ally through a lot of tough times, was the one who suffered the most, her and my poor Granny Linster. The first time I tried to introduce Minny to drugs was when we went for our usual Sunday visit to Granny Millie's. She was shocked to say the least. She out and out refused to have anything to do with it, no matter how hard I tried to convince her.

"It's only hash" was my biggest argument.

"It's not like it's going to kill you."

She stood her ground though, stating clearly that it was evil.

"You are inviting the devil into our lives" she said.

I tried to brush her off, but I still felt that knot of fear in my stomach, all the same.

I knew she was more than likely right, but I refused to admit it. I would not give up on this new feeling (of freedom/control) so easily. That was until I got slapped in the face with the absolute proof. Then there was no more denying. It started after the 2nd or 3rd time I tried to convince Minny to get high with me.

Finally she caved. We went behind the old barn. I pulled out my little stash of hash. I did exactly what I had been taught to do by my fellow

155

dope smokers. Things seemed to be fine at first; we were having a great time.

The higher we got, the stranger Minny began to act. I tried to ignore her at first, but she was definitely scaring me. She started to say and see all kinds of crazy things. She was whispering about how we shouldn't have done this, and we were going to regret it. I tried to calm her down, but it was not working. I don't know if I was more afraid of the way she was acting, or the trouble I was going to be in if we were caught. This was something I wasn't expecting.

She then began to tell me of how she could feel the evil starting to surround us. I had to admit it, as much as I hated to, I could feel it too. I was not arguing with her because I knew what evil felt like. I had felt it before. The more she talked about seeing these things, the more I started to see them too. Suddenly everything seemed to be cast in grey, a sure sign the devil was around. I was scared as I could see the black shadows coming toward us as we tried to hide.

There was nothing to protect us. I was so high, I thought for a split second it was just my imagination, but at the same time I wasn't taking the chance to find out if it was. We got up and started to run. We ran like we'd never run before. I thought my lungs were going to explode in my chest, but I knew we had to outrun those demons, or whatever they were. I was so sure by this point that I wasn't imagining it. They were real, just as real as I was running from them. Just as quickly as they were hot on our tail, they were gone. Minny warned me though, that it wasn't the last we had seen or heard from them.

I got a chill up my spine as she spoke. She was so right, even more right than either one of us would realize until it was too late. We had done something terribly wrong, and the only one who could ever really help us, was the only one they were after. Like I said before, once that door is opened, there is no closing it. It didn't take us long to hear from those demons again. It was the way we heard from them that shocked me and the whole family the most.

It was a few days later when my mother got a frantic call from my Granny Milly. She would not say what it was about, but we had to go there immediately.

"The whole family" she screamed at my mother on the phone.

"Do not leave anyone home alone no matter what."

Even my mother looked afraid, which made us kids more frightened. I hadn't forgotten what had happened, but I never suspected it would have anything to do with our urgent need to be present at my Granny Millie's house.

Her whole house was in an uproar when we arrived. The kids were all ushered outside so the adults could whisper alone for the first half hour or so. When you are waiting for some horrible news, a half hour is a life time. It was almost like waiting for a punishment you knew was coming, but were so afraid to get. My curiosity was killing be, but at the same time, I didn't want to know what was going on. My gut told me that I would be in big trouble if I let on that I knew anything that was going on, or if I told anyone of what had happened to Minny and me.

Finally after what seemed like an eternity, all of us kids were called into the house. You could have heard a pin drop. Everyone looked so ashamed, or at least they did in my mind. I think that was just my own feeling of shame I felt, but would or did not want to face it.

"Well," Granny Milly said, *"Something very bad has happened."*

No one even wanted to ask her, so we waited for her to continue talking.

"Someone has invited the devil into our lives" she said.

Everyone looked as shocked as I felt. I just stood there holding my breath, unable to move. I was terrified my mother would find out it was me.

I mean, was this even possible? I had to think that maybe I had heard her wrong. I wanted to think maybe it wasn't possible, just an old superstition. But I knew it was possible. I was even more shocked at what I heard next.

"The devil" Granny Milly announced, *"has followed Granny Linster home."*

The silence was almost deafening, and it seemed to go on forever after this announcement. Finally Granny Linster came out of the bedroom after to give us the whole story. The story that was unbelievable, almost too unbelievable, but I knew my Granny Linster would never lie. That story she told us is something that is burned into my mind, even to this very day.

"My End is Near"

As the story was told, Granny Linster was on her way home from church the night before. She was walking down the old railroad tracks, as she had done every night for the last 30 years or so. She described how clear the sky was when she left the church, making me feel as if I was the one who was walking on the tracks. As she got down the tracks, she could hear a soft sound behind her. She looked behind her, but couldn't see anything, and just continued walking.

The sound got louder. She began to realize it was the sound of horses trotting behind her. She thought this more than a bit strange. Not too many people she knew would have their horses out so late at night. She also didn't know anyone who would ride their horses on the tracks, and risk injuring one of the horse's legs. The sound, she said, seemed to get louder and louder with every step she took.

Her stomach was all tied up in knots. She began to feel the evil, she said, and the air became foggy with a mist that clung to her skin. She was truly getting frightened by now, and began to walk faster and faster. Pointing her bony finger at us, she said, almost in a whisper, *"The faster I walked the louder and faster the hooves came behind me."*

I was very frightened at this point, just listening to her.

"I tried to look behind me," she said, *"but there was nothing there, only blackness, which scared me even more."*

She was an old lady, but even so, she began to run as fast as she could. She knew every tie on that track, but stumbled on every one of them on the way home anyway. She was terrified that whatever it was, it would catch up with her on those train tracks. I wouldn't blame her. I was terrified just listening to her.

"Finally," she said, out of breath, just like she was reliving the event over again in her mind, *"I reached my house."*

She ran inside, and slammed the door, hoping that whatever it was would go away.

No one had locks in our town, so she grabbed her old rocking chair and put it up under the door handle, securely barring the door. Then she was really quiet for a while. It was only a few minutes, but it seemed like hours. Granny Linster's voice got really quiet as she began to tell us the rest of the story.

"I sat back in my chair," she said, *"and I could hear the breathing from this thing. The breathing was so loud, I swear to God, even the walls were breathing."*

I never, in all my short life, heard my granny swearing to God. That was a sin, almost like taking His name in vain.

"I began to pray to the Lord, Jesus like never before," she said, *"And I must have had His presence there with me, because I fell asleep right there in the chair."*

I thought that that was the end of the story, and gave a little sigh of relief. That was not to be the case. Much to everyone's surprise, the story got even worse. Granny Linster finally started talking again. I hated it sometimes, when it took her forever to say what she had to say.

"I opened the door, the next morning," she said, *"To go get some eggs out of the chicken coop for breakfast and there it was!"*

"What?!" I felt like screaming.

It seemed to take her forever to continue once again. No one dared breathe a word. We all sat on the edge of our seats. A horseshoe was at her doorstep. The worst thing in the world, as far as our little town was concerned.

"It was right there staring me in the face!" was the way she put it.

A horseshoe was an old superstition in our little town, until this point. Everyone I knew had one hanging above their door to keep the evil out. If you ever found one on your step, like my Granny Linster did, you were in big trouble. The devil had followed her home. Surely this would be the death of her. She was frightened like I had never seen her before; almost as white as the fresh fallen snow was the color of her face.

"My end is near," she said, *"My end is near."*

***

CHAPTER 20

Minny

Guilt is a terrible thing to burden yourself with and carry around. My guilt after what happened to Granny Linster was overwhelming and all-consuming. I guess in my child's mind I really had way too much guilt. All of the stuff that happened to me over such a short lifetime was just too much to bear. I was finally at my breaking point. I just didn't realize it yet.

Self-Promises

Once the devil followed Granny Linster home, I decided to never touch drugs again. I would never be able to live with myself if something was to happen to her. I made this promise to God, kind of as a bargaining chip.

My promises however, were extremely short-lived. I did try, but dealing with my mother was just more than I could bear, and drugs seemed to be the only thing to calm that accumulated rage inside of me. I couldn't tell my friends I stopped or why, so I told them I thought my mother was on to me. They accepted that, thank God, without question.

I truly had no intention of starting to smoke drugs again, but the devil, I really believe, knows your weak spots. He knew mine, and made sure I had every opportunity to get high. I went for about a week before I started smoking hash again. Even as I smoked it, I said a silent prayer to God to forgive me. I was hoping he would. It seemed like everything was so totally out of control in my life. I needed to do something.

Things at home seemed to get a lot worse. I'm not sure if it was because I had a clear mind, or the stress of what had happened to Granny

Linster. I could feel the tension mounting, until finally I could not take it anymore. I went up the road to hang out. By this point, I had everyone smoking, so I caved. I was very disappointed with myself, but it was better than dealing with my grim life at home. I was back on that destructive path I loved so much. Even the guilt wasn't so bad. I was able to think about it for a minute, and then forget it for a while.

So I started to get high again. At first it was just the once, and I said my little prayer. When nothing bad happened to Granny Linster, I jumped right in again, full force. It was like I never stopped. I always began by saying a little prayer, but after a couple of days, I forgot about that too, and devolved right back to my old ways. I think it was only a few days later when things started to happen, things that were unexplainable.

Suicide Attempt

Then one day everything came to a head. Minny was acting very strangely since the incident that happened to us. I always made it a point to call her right after school (when I wasn't grounded of course). Just like clockwork, every day she would answer the phone, and we would talk until one of us got in trouble.

It was usually me who would get in trouble first for being on the phone. We would hang up, but it would happen exactly the same way the very next day. Lately though, Minnie wasn't answering the phone, or she would answer, and tell me she had to go. I knew she was smoking hash, but at the time I didn't connect the 2. All I knew was something was definitely not right. Right after she started smoking hash, she began avoiding me.

As for me, I began to have these really strange dreams. I kept dreaming I was running down this mountain, and a big black horse was chasing me. Every time, just before he got me, I would wake up. I felt I couldn't tell anyone about the dreams, but they left me with such a feeling of dread. The feeling was so strong, sometimes the next day it made me physically sick.

It seemed to me that the more days that went by, the more distant Minny became. This dream became stronger, until I was sitting on the edge, waiting for this big black horse.

One night, everything came to a head. It was like I suddenly knew it was time for me to go. Minny had not talked to me for 2 days at this point. I wasn't really worried about her, but whenever her name was mentioned, I got a sinking feeling in the pit of my stomach. This day was worse than most. No matter how hard I tried, I could not get Minny out of my mind. I came home from school, and was in trouble as usual, but I really couldn't understand what my mother was saying. I was so preoccupied with Minny. I was grounded once again, so there was no way of even calling her. I really felt desperate, but I had no idea why.

It would not take too long to find out. I got this really strong feeling, after sitting upstairs waiting for the night to pass. It was about 8 PM. I could feel this anxiety building in my
stomach, until I could no longer stand it. It was literally taking every ounce of my energy not to go and call Minny. I was very afraid for her. I had no idea why. I knew what the consequences would be if I was to pick up the phone to call, but I felt I had no choice. I just had to do it, damn the consequences!

My mother had a phone in her room. Did I dare go try to use it? I knew I had to, but what if I was jumping the gun, or worse yet what if something was happening? What if I really needed to tell someone that she was in danger? That's what my gut was telling me. My gut, it seemed to me, was rarely wrong.

Once I was utterly convinced I could no longer ignore this feeling, I decided to call

Minny, even though I knew I would be dead if I was caught. My mother was out in the yard, thank God, when I dared venture out of my room. I was so afraid. I could feel the heat rising to my cheeks as I tried to open the door as quietly as I could. I dialed the number, and prayed for Minny to answer.

I knew the minute she answered the phone that something was very wrong with her. I tried to sound like I didn't know anything, as I asked her how she was doing. Her voice was very slurred. It wasn't what she was saying.

All I could make out was, *"I'm sick of the devil trying to get my soul and I want to be with God."*

Utter panic and terror is an understatement of what I felt as I knew my feeling was right.

"Put Granny Milly on the phone." I said, after I could feel her fading from this plane, and onto the next. She refused, no matter how hard I tried to convince her that I wouldn't say anything. I knew I had to tell someone, but I didn't want it to be my mother. I knew she would chalk it up to one of my lies, and probably beat me instead of trying to save Minnie's life.

After all, according to my mother, I could stand on a stack of Bibles and lie. I decided to call my aunt, who lived right next door to my Granny Milly. I prayed as I told Minny I had to go, because I was grounded. I prayed so hard that she would not die in the time it took me to call someone for help. She was so out of it, I don't think she even knew it was me talking to her on the phone. I felt terrible for letting her go, but I knew I had to do something.

I dialed my aunt as quickly as I could. She answered on the first ring. I don't even think I gave her a chance to say hello, when I started yelling about Minny.

"She's taken an overdose!"

164

I was screaming into the phone, feeling my head beginning to pulsate from all of the pressure of screaming. I totally forgot about being caught by my mother. I don't even remember if my aunt even asked who had taken the overdose. She just automatically knew it was Minny.

"I'll call an ambulance." she said, with a peculiar kind of calm in her voice, almost like she had been sitting, waiting for my desperate call.

"Go and tell your mother, but first call Minny back and keep her on the phone."

I was like a robot. I did exactly as I was told. I was thinking the whole time about how I was ever going to get out of this one. I felt responsible. If only I had never tried to force those awful drugs on her. I can't even remember calling Minny back, but there she was on the phone, telling me how she couldn't take it anymore.

"I'm sick of feeling evil around me.", she said.

My guilt almost choked the life out of me at that moment in time. I had Minny on the phone as I was yelling out to my mother. She was right about my lying. The first words out of her mouth when she came up the stairs were, *"What the hell do you think you are doing?"*

"The phone just kept ringing and ringing," I said, *"so I thought I had better answer it."*

The lie came almost too easily. I thought for sure she was going to completely lose it from the look in her eyes. I must have looked panicked. She grabbed the phone out of my hands without saying a word. She handed the phone back to me after a bit, and told me, no matter what do not hang up the phone. Then she was gone.

I heard the car racing up the road. I knew this was probably the most serious situation I had ever had to face in my whole life. As messed up as Minny was, she never did try to hang up on me. I could feel her fading over the phone, her life slipping away with every word she spoke. I never felt so helpless or hopeless in my entire life.

"There's no Way They are Taking Me Alive!"

It seemed like it took a million years for the ambulance and police to get there. She had the door to her bedroom barricaded, and was not letting anyone in. She just wanted to die. I knew exactly how she felt. I was trying to convince her to open the door to get help. I was yelling at her through the phone, but I knew it was no use. She was just as stubborn as I was.

They called the fire department to bust the door down, but Minny was so messed up.

She said *"There's no way they're taking me alive!"*

What she was planning even shocked me, the one who always had a messed-up plan.

"Minnie, you mean so much to me and I won't be able to face things without you." I said.

This was one of the very few times I would ever speak from my heart, but it was the truth. Nothing seemed to matter to her by this point, not even my precious Granny Milly. She was saying goodbye to me as the fire department broke down the door. Then suddenly, the phone went dead. I thought for sure she was dead. I started to sob uncontrollably.

I think I must have gone a little bit insane that day. How could I take much more? I must have fallen asleep like that, with the dead phone clutched in my hand on my mother's bed. I woke up with my eye twitching, which was a sure sign that someone died or was about to. I had the feeling that someone was staring at me. It was completely dark. I had almost forgotten what

happened such a short time ago.

The memories came flooding back very quickly, bringing tears to my eyes once again. I could not understand why no one had bothered to wake me up, and why the house was so quiet.

I got out of bed as quietly as I could, fearing that my mother was waiting on the other side of the door with her belt. The door, I knew, would give me away as soon as I opened it, but I knew I could not stay there.

To my surprise, there was no one there. In fact, the house was completely empty. I knew this was not a good sign. Our house was never completely empty. I made my way down to the kitchen, feeling along the walls, afraid to turn on the hall light, in case my mother was sleeping on the couch. I had no idea what time it was. I felt like I was trapped in a 3rd dimension.

Once I reached the kitchen, I tried to look at the clock without turning on the light, but I knew it was no use. I even tried to climb on the counter and feel the hands of the clock with my fingers, but it was hopeless, I was never good at telling time.

Finally, after way too much guessing, I decided I had no choice but to turn on the light. I was very surprised to find it was almost 10 o'clock at night. Where was everyone, I wondered? I was beginning to panic, but I hate to admit it, I was also a bit happy. I thought maybe I would be lucky, and they had all died. There was no way I was going back to sleep as much as I wished they were all dead. The thought of being alone scared me more than anything.

My First Ever Note

I sat at the table for at least 15 minutes before I noticed the note. I was surprised to see it. I had never received a note from anyone before. There it was, in big letters, my name: *"Lexis"*. I was almost afraid to open the folded paper, but I knew I would never stop thinking about it if I didn't. I slowly took the paper from the coffee cup that was holding it up, and began to read it. I must admit I was a little disappointed when I opened it. It was only a few short lines, nothing like I had pictured a note I received would be like.

The note read, *"We have gone to the hospital, Lexis. There has been a terrible tragedy. We have Vin and Joe with us. Ann is at the neighbors. We will be home in a little while. You had better be in your own bed."*

I knew this was not a request but a warning. I was so sure Minny was dead and almost felt like defying my mother by staying up. I also knew what the consequences would be if I was to do something as stupid as that. I would pay, no matter who had died. So I sat quietly in the living room, waiting as every set of headlights came down the road, to see if it was my mother. Every time I would see the headlights, I would run upstairs, my heart pounding in my throat, trying to pretend I was sleeping. I knew I couldn't call anyone, so it was going to be a long night.

It was around 1AM when they finally came home. I knew they weren't going to get me up to let me know what was going on, so I had to strain to hear, trying to at least catch a little bit of the conversation. It was eerily quiet, quieter than I had ever heard it. Why did she have to overdose?

***

CHAPTER 21

Granny Linster

I must have fallen asleep listening, because I woke up in the morning with that same awful feeling of ice water being thrown in my face. My mother was angry, but it wasn't her usual anger I noticed as she dragged me out of bed pulling me by my hair. I'm not sure how I knew it was different, but my senses told me so.

Mother's Tears

"Get downstairs you dirty tramps!" she yelled at my sister and me, before our eyes were even fully open. We didn't feel the cold of the morning as we scurried down the stairs. The icy cold fear of what was about to happen was all I felt, deep in the pit of my stomach. I thought for sure we were going to get the worst beating of our lives after waking up like that. Instead my mother came down the stairs behind us and sat at the table. All of us kids were lined up, holding
our breath, waiting for the worst to happen, when something happened that surprised us all.

My mother sat at the table, put her head in her hands, and began to sob uncontrollably. What a strange sight it was! I think we were all in a state of shock for a few minutes, because no one moved. Finally, Ann moved toward her, and started patting her on the shoulder. She was braver then me at that moment. I had learned from previous experiences not to try to give my mother any affection, nor to ask for any.

None of us dared ask what was going on. I instantly began to think of Minny, and started crying too. Silent tears fell down my cheeks. No matter how hard I tried, I could not stop them. Before too long, Vin and Joe joined Ann in patting my mother on the back and shoulders, but I still couldn't move. I had seen my mother shed a few tears now and then, but it actually hurt my heart to hear her sobbing like that.

I'm not sure how long my mother was crying, but my legs were beginning to ache from standing there, as she slowly raised her head.

"The devil," she said, *"has our family in his clutches."*

I wasn't sure what she was talking about, but I felt afraid, very afraid. She didn't ask us to sit. I was glad, because suddenly the room and house seemed to be filled with a coldness that chilled me to the bone. Even though I felt like I was choking, I found my voice and dared to ask her about Minny.

"Is Minny dead?" I had to ask.

She looked at me with a blank stare, almost like she was seeing straight into my soul. I just knew she knew that I was the one that had brought this terrible curse on our family. I really hated waiting for an answer. I felt like going up to my mother and shaking the life out of her, just to get her to respond.

"No." she finally said, and that was it for another 10 minutes or so.

When she spoke next, I felt the blood drain from my face, and everything began

to go black. She began to speak, and as she did, I felt as though it was me living the terrible nightmare of Granny Linster and Minny.

"Minny," she said, speaking directly to me, looking right into my eyes with what I perceived as pure hatred.

"Minny jumped out of her bedroom window when the fire department broke her door down."

I was holding my breath. I knew there was no way she could survive that fall. It was 3 floors up.

"She is in the hospital with a broken leg," My mother said, *"and she will be in the hospital for a while."*

"Wow!", I thought, *"I wonder why she is so upset over that. At least Minny is still alive."*

That however, was just the beginning of the night.

"Once they were all at the hospital," my mother began to tell us, *"Minny was out of control. She kept saying the devil was at work and we could do nothing to stop it. They were giving her drugs to calm her down after they pumped her stomach, but no matter how much they gave her she would not sleep. The doctors were completely puzzled by this. She had enough drugs in her system to knock out a horse. After about an hour, she started to go almost hysterical."* my mother said.

"Here he comes! Here he comes!" she said over and over again, until she was screaming out of control. We were trying to get her under control when the call came in."*

The pause she made after this statement, and the one minute was almost killing me. I don't think it was curiosity, but fear of what she was going to say next.

"A woman got run over by a horse," my mother said, *"She was dead when she arrived at the hospital. That woman was Granny Linster. She got run over on her way home from church."*

That's when I began to black out. I could feel my body began to sweat cold sweat from my toes right up through the top of my head. Black spots started swimming in front of my eyes just before I fainted. I think (for me and the whole family), the shock was almost too much to bear.

It was much worse for me. I had caused this awful thing that had happened to both Minny and Granny Linster. I felt like I was in some kind of dream (nightmare) state, waiting for someone to throw cold water on my face and wake me up.

The Unexplained

Apparently it was a horse and buggy that ran her over. They were from someone's farm up the road. There were so many unanswered questions. It was all too strange for the family to absorb. Once the police found out who owned the horse and buggy, they were just as stunned as the rest of us.

They told the police in the official report that Paul, the owner, had finished his farm work at about 7 PM. The police had asked him if he was using his horse and buggy.

"Not the buggy." Paul explained to the police.

Paul confirmed that the buggy was never used, except for (relatively rare) town celebrations. The horses were old pit horses which he would never have considered hooking up to the buggy due to their age. He had other special horses for that job. He swore on the Bible when he went before the judge. He swore that he had locked the old pit horses up in their stalls. There was absolutely no way they could get out on their own.

He did confess that when he got wind of what happened from one of the neighbors, he felt very uneasy and went out to check his stables. When he opened the door to go outside, standing there right in front of him were the 2 pit horses with the wagon attached to them. He went out to the stables to figure out how they had escaped, but the stable door still had the same padlock on it that he had personally put on the night before.

No one else had a key. That's when he phoned the police. The police had no other choice but to believe him after they had searched his property and stables. The police could not find any explanation. Charges could not be filed by the police, nor do I think they even wanted to file charges. They were, after all, men of science, and could find no logical explanation for this.

Rituals

In our small town (with our traditional focus on religion), we had a few rituals that had to be carried out when someone went to the other side, so their soul could rest in peace.

Due to the mysterious circumstances of Granny Linster's death, these practices were even more important. The devil, according to all of the adults in our family, was fighting us every step of the way. He wanted Granny Linster's soul, and would go to any lengths to get it.

Whenever someone went to the other side (like Granny Linster) we always had the wake in the living room. All the windows had to be left open so the person's soul could go to heaven. We had to cover all of the mirrors in the house as, according to our beliefs, the next one to look in the mirror would die within the year.

We also had to stop the clock in the living room where Granny Linster's body was, or more bad luck would surely befall the family. The devil was at work, and doing everything he could ensure Granny Linster's soul was going to be his. The windows, when we opened

them would slam shut with such a violent force, my Granny Milly made us kids stand by them to keep them open so the devil couldn't capture her soul.

Against all possibilities, the clock kept chiming every hour on the hour WITHOUT BATTERIES! It finally got to the point where my grandfather, who didn't have a violent bone in his body, got so freaked out, he took the clock out to the barn and smashed it to smithereens. Every mirror that was covered in the house was also taken outside, and buried.

This was done after the sheets continuously kept coming off them. From what I can remember, not one of them was ever dug up.

Finally, after the 3 day wake and the trip to the church for the funeral, we heard the sound of thunder in the distance a sure sign Granny Linster had made it to the other side. We had once again, according to Granny Milly, definitely defeated the devil, and all of his evil forces. We knew Granny Linster had made it to heaven.

***

CHAPTER 22

The Decision

After the death of Granny Linster, I knew for certain that it was absolutely my time to go. My life had become a living hell. The whole sordid story of Minny getting her first taste of drugs through me came to out. Now the whole family looked at me and scorned me because I was a "drug addict" according to them. I didn't even know what that meant at the time. It took me many years to finally figure out what it meant and the truth was that they were right. Even back then, it was the beginning down the road to addiction for me.

She didn't tell anyone, it was the doctor she was seeing in the nut house that ratted me right out. I don't think he ever realized how much trouble he caused me. I don't think I was ever so miserable in my entire life. Every chance my mother got, she would slap me and tell me over and over again how much she hated me. Her rage had me fearing for my life, especially when she would tell me how she wished I had never been born. I was terrified, thinking that she was going to kill me. Then another plan began to fill my mind. A plan I became so obsessed with, it frightened me to no end.

A couple of weeks after Granny Linster died, Minny got out of the hospital, and came to live with us. Tragically, she wasn't the same Minny, not the same Minny at all. It wasn't her looks. She still looked the same. It was her whole personality. She was never the same after that overdose. The doctors told Granny Milly that Minny had suffered brain damage from all of the drugs she had consumed.

Minny had begun to have all of these rituals she had to perform before she ate, or went outside, etc. She could not look at herself in the mirror. To ask her to write her own name would cause a fit of hysterics and hyperventilating. In fact, when I think about it now, over the decades since this has happened, Minny has gotten worse, not better.

I felt so, so guilty, and was reminded by the universe every day of the terrible thing I had
done. I was not only reminded by my mother, but also by almost everyone else in my family, everyone that is except for Granny Milly. The very few times when I did get a chance to be alone with Minny (I was forbidden to be alone with her and watched like a hawk), I really did try to apologize.

Minny on her end acted like she had no idea what I was talking about. Maybe it was just too horrible, or too shameful for her to even think about or remember. Maybe the brain damage had wiped out major parts of her memory.

Things for me were on a downward spiral. I had no idea how long I had been grounded, but once again, it felt like a lifetime. There were no drugs for me to numb the pain during this time, so everything seemed to be multiplied by 10. It really overwhelmed me. In fact, it got so bad, I began to have what I found out later were panic attacks. My anger and hatred for my mother and stepfather grew and grew.

Not So Little Thoughts

I began to have these little thoughts. At first that's all they were, just small thoughts in my messed-up brain. I pushed them way to the back of my mind since I knew they were pure evil. No matter how much they kept creeping into my mind, I knew I had to avoid thinking about them. I did my best to ignore them. It didn't quite work out that way. I guess my mother was right. I had the mark of the devil. Once I had that, there was no hope for me, or people like me. I was said and believed to be destined for a life of trouble and hardship.

I should get back to these thoughts, or at least what started out as a little thought. It was always just a simple thought, until it became an obsession. Before long, I was making some crazy and destructive plan. Once this planning process started there was no stopping me. Was I driven by evil? I sometimes wondered.

What was this thought that began to overtake me in my every waking moment? It is so sad to say. I am almost too ashamed to write it. Not only because of the thought, but because I came so close to actually carrying it out, as absolutely insanely crazy as it was. I had decided in my sick, emotionally messed-up mind that I was never going to escape my mother's rage. Additionally, I would never get away from my stepfather's sexual abuse. I felt like I was at the end of a very short rope, hanging off the edge of a very steep cliff.

Nothing seemed to be working for me. I couldn't even kill myself properly! I spent nights awake, contemplating this. I knew I had to do it, no matter what the cost or consequences. I had to kill my mother and stepfather. I wasn't sure how, but I knew it had to be done. I had just read the book, *"The Burning Bed"*, and actually considered sending them up in flames. The only thing that stopped me was how guilty I would have felt if anyone else got hurt, especially my sister, Ann.

What I did know was that I definitely had to do it when they were sleeping. I was strong when it came to beating up my friends, but my mother, in my eyes, seemed like the Incredible Hulk. I was terrified of her. It was something she instilled in me right from birth. All kinds of ideas formed in my mind once I made that faithful decision. They kept coming for many days after that. I found myself being so torn one minute. I was so afraid to even think about it, and the next minute it would be all I was thinking about.

I would find myself thinking about stealing a butcher's knife from the kitchen, and hiding it under my carpet. All this, just to wait for my opportunity to kill those bastards. In my mind, they left me with no choice. This, I think, was one of the most confusing times in my life. I wasn't sure what I was going to do, but my obsession became so bad, I was seriously losing sleep over it. I lay there night after night, waiting and listening for my mother and stepfather to close their door to their room, and go to sleep.

I would find myself waiting, only to chicken out at the last minute. The next day, I would
wake up so angry and frustrated at myself, I began to take it out on everyone around me, making their life a living Hell (like mine was).

I don't think my mother and stepfather ever had any idea how close that they actually came to dying. I felt like I was a walking time-bomb waiting to explode. This went on for a couple of months at least. I remember 1 minute it seemed like it was summer, and the next minute it was almost Halloween. I was ready to carry out my plan.

<u>Death is Near</u>

I decided I was going to wait until my mother was sleeping on the couch. I would stab my stepfather first, and then deal with her. I remember wishing I was stronger and older, so I
could hold her captive and torture her the way she was torturing me. As fate would have it, nothing ever happens for me quite as I plan. I did try to stab my stepfather on devil's night, but I just couldn't do it.

I stood over his bed with the butcher's knife raised above him, with all intentions of carrying out my evil deed, but I couldn't do it. Why I didn't do it is the most bizarre part of all. I heard a voice. I know, and will swear to this day it was the voice of God.

178

I was standing over my stepfather, crying like I had never cried before. Every fiber in my body was telling me what I was about to do was so wrong. I closed my eyes, and was about to strike when I heard someone say my name. I thought at first it was just my imagination or worse yet, my mother. I closed my eyes again, and got ready again. That time I knew I heard someone say my name. I also knew I was alone in the room except for my sleeping stepfather, who was

about to have his life brutally taken away.

I was terrified by this point, not knowing who this voice belonged to, but at the same time, my every instinct told me that I did know. I stood there, actually talking to God in my mind. I told him I couldn't take it anymore. I was doing this to get away from this awful life.

Did He answer me? Not in the way you would think, but I felt Him fill my body with such a feeling of warmth and love, that I suddenly realized the foolishness of what I was

about to do. I dropped the knife and went back to bed, not feeling like I was as evil as my mother had told and convinced me over the years. I knew I still had to get out and get away from the insanity, but this time I knew I would get out.

All Hallows Eve

That was the first correct decision I had made. I was caught in a kind of a time warp. The next day was Halloween. I woke up still feeling that love and warmth. There was no way I wanted it to go away. Like all good things, it had to come to an end. I did feel better in a way, knowing that I was not as alone as I thought I was.

I always hated Halloween. That, according to my Granny Linster, was when the dead or dearly departed got their only chance to mix with the living. When she said things like that, it scared the crap out of me. I also hated it, I think, because we were so poor. Every year was like a repeat of the last. We didn't have costumes like the other kids. For as long as I could remember, we had to wear white garbage bags with the bottoms cut out of them for our arms to fit in like sleeves, and bright red lipstick smeared all over the front to look like blood.

This year was unfortunately no different. Even though we were all getting older. I went to call for Liza, one of my best friends at the time. She knew about my situation, and how truly unhappy I was. She was trying to find a way out for me, almost as desperately as I was. She was Marley's niece and lived right next door to me. So many a time she had come to help me babysit even though she didn't drink with me. We were as close as two friends could be. That night, she finally had a solution. To say I was shocked when she told me of her plan, is an understatement. We were actually supposed to carry it out that night, but once again, circumstances would not allow it.

Liza thankfully, knew how embarrassing it was for me to go out trick or treating with a plastic bag as a costume and red lipstick all over my face. She decided to do something about it. She still had her mask from the year before, and gave it to me to wear, along with an old hunting shirt and a cane. I felt like a million dollars, not that anyone would make fun of me, at least not to my face. I was getting dressed as slowly as I could, trying to savor every bit of the experience of this real costume.

A Plan is Devised

As I was dressing, she told me of her plan. Liza had an aunt, Michelle was her name. We used to babysit for her. Usually it was Liza who did the babysitting, but Michelle would always call my mother, and tell her she needed me to watch her kids, even though she didn't. All just so I could get a little break away from the toxic life of insanity that I lived in. She always paid both Liza and I for babysitting, even when money was very tight for her, and she couldn't afford it.

I never told Michelle what was going on, but I knew she had seen the bruises on me like everyone else. The only difference between her and everyone else was that she would never ask what happened. She just let me know that she would help me if ever I needed her. She never asked and I never told, but Liza did, and even though that was only half of the story, she knew I had to get out. Liza never knew the shame I felt in telling her even the small bits that I did. I knew she could be trusted, knowing only part of my story, although we did get into the occasional fist fight.

Back to her plan. It wasn't as if Liza asked Michelle. Michelle was actually the one who came up with the plan. What a plan it was too! I knew it just had to work, not just because I was desperate, but because it was so, so good.

It was supposed to happen that night, October 31st, but my temper once again got the best of me. We were supposed to go out for Halloween. Liza and I left early to go to Michelle's so she could help me escape my life.

It seemed almost too perfect, and of course it was. One big thing that stopped me from carrying out my plan was my sister, Ann. She had to come with me, not only because of my mother, but also because she was afraid, and I was her protector. After a lot of brainstorming, Liza and figured we would just ditch Ann outside of my soon-to-be former home, and make a run for it. Like they say, Murphy's Law kicked in and whatever could go wrong, did.

I was actually worried about where I was going to go. I had never really thought it through before. Well yes, I thought about it, but that was when I thought it was never going to happen. This time was different and I knew it. Deep inside me, I just knew. I decided I was going to go to my real father's house. Even though I felt like we were strangers, I knew I would not be turned away. I would tell him anything I needed to, so that wasn't going to happen. I was even willing to tell him about my stepfather's sexual abuse if I had to.

Then the next thing that happened seemed to dash all my hopes of ever escaping mother's wrath. I thank God, even at that age I was a quick thinker. We were walking up the road collecting all the candy we could, when someone came up behind my sister. They didn't recognize us because of the masks we borrowed from Liza. The guy tried to grab my sister's bag. This

was pretty common back then. I however, was so pumped up on adrenaline with the thought of getting out of this nasty little town, I just freaked out.

I didn't even think twice when I heard my sister scream. I just reacted and started to beat the culprit over the head, until I felt someone grab me from behind and pull me off. This was my excuse for dropping my sister at home. She was quite terrified by this point, even though I beat the guy into submission. We took her home. I gave her most of the candy I had, just to make her feel better. I knew she would tell my mother the whole story so I just dropped her off at the driveway and continued on my way.

Murphy Has This Law....

I was after all, on my way to freedom and felt no need to go in and explain. Liza was concerned but I just brushed her off.

"What if something goes wrong?" she asked me.

"Impossible!" I thought and even said out loud.

As usual, I was wrong. We arrived at Michelle's, and she was ready to go. I was so excited, I puked. Could this really be coming to an end, I thought. No it wasn't, or at least not that night. Michelle jumped into her car with as much anticipation as I felt. She turned over the key. It made a few sluggish noises, then nothing. I could feel the car getting smaller and smaller, as she tried again and again to start it. Nothing seemed to work no

182

matter how hard we tried to get it going. She even got me to hide in her house when she got one of the neighbors to try to boost her.

I was once again in big trouble for one of my stupid plans. I was afraid to go home because it was almost 9PM and I knew there would be a lot of questions I'd have to answer. I had also been drinking rum, partly to relieve the anxiety, and partly to celebrate the fact I was leaving. Michelle assured me over and over again, once she had seen how upset I was, that she would get me out of that hell I called home.

I did believe her, but I was too overwhelmed with disappointment at the time to think she would be able to do it. I went home, but it was nothing like I had anticipated. My mother wasn't

even home so I just went straight to bed. The next day I woke up thinking that the night before was just a dream. It wasn't. I went to school, bribing Ann the whole way so she wouldn't say

anything about my dropping her off. To my surprise she told me that because I had saved her, she wouldn't say a word. Usually I doubted her, this time I knew I could trust her.

Goodbye Time

Once I arrived at school, I met Liza. I was still carrying the shame of crying like a baby the night before, so I tried to avoid her. She was Liza though, and never got discouraged about small things like people avoiding her.

"You will meet me after school." she wrote in a note she passed me.

"I can't." I wrote back, but she kept writing.

Then she wrote something to catch my attention.

"Michelle bought a new battery and alternator," she wrote and she said *"whenever you are ready."* I think she wrote, *"You are ready now, and even if you are not, it is time for you to go."*

I thought all day about what she had said. The fact that I was willing to kill my mother and stepfather made me realize she was right. It was time for me to go. I would make my

great escape soon.

***

CHAPTER 23

Anywhere But Here

The day had finally come and I was sick to my stomach. I met Liza after school. We began to plan again. This time, I wasn't quite as cocky as I had been the last couple of times. I was actually starting to realize the seriousness and non-reversibility of my situation and decision.

Good vs. Evil

To me it was a battle from within my soul, the good against the evil. Who was going to win? Only time would tell. I felt the pressure from Liza. She was expecting me to leave just like that, but I knew it could (and probably would) not be that easy. This time, I was determined to make sure there were no hiccups and that I would get out before it was too late.

Interestingly, school seemed to go all too quickly that day. Not too many days were like that. Usually the days seemed to drag on so long that I would fall asleep in class. This would invariably ensure that I would be receiving the strap whipping from the principal. For once in my life, I didn't want to think or to face Liza and her thousands of questions about why that day wasn't a good one to leave. It was the day after Halloween. I felt like I had missed my chance.

Liza however, wouldn't take no for an answer. I began to have all of these really strange thoughts that made absolutely no sense to me. I was thinking about what I was going to do about clothes, something I had never even considered before. It wasn't like I actually had good clothes! Most of them were hand-me-downs. It was just a part of my growing up poor.

I was thinking about it so much that I actually tried to use it as my excuse to not leave, or so I told Liza. Always the quick thinker, Liza came up with a solution very quickly. She could, I think, feel my anxiety and told me of a new plan.

"First," she said, *"every morning when you get up for school, you need to double up on your layers of clothes."*

This seemed almost ridiculous to me, and I told her. Because of the cold weather, I was already doubling up on my layers of clothes. I misunderstood her. She meant I had to wear 3 pairs of pants, not 2. She expected me to do the same with my sweaters and socks.

Every morning she would meet me in the bathroom to take the extra clothes. I asked her every day what the rest of her plan was, but every day she just told me to wait and see. I thought I was going to get caught. I didn't, but each morning the fear I had going down the stairs and out the door made me puke.

Once Thursday finally came, Liza let me know of the rest of her plan. It was almost too much for me to take, the fear and excitement all at the same time. I was grounded at home, so I knew that saying I was needed to go babysit was absolutely out of the question. I really had no idea what she was planning.

Once she did tell me, I knew it was very risky, but I was not left with much choice. My mother could keep me grounded for a very long time. It seemed to be something she actually really enjoyed, almost too much.

We had a new dog by this point, one that I really didn't like. He was so nasty and smelly. Every night after supper, my mother would let the dog out and sometimes he would come back, sometimes he wouldn't. It was always my job to go looking for that dumb dog, chasing him all over the neighborhood to bring him back. I remember once coming home and telling my mother in tears that the dog was impossible to catch. He ran around me in the cold night for almost an hour before I gave up. To my mother, this was unacceptable. After a good beating with the belt, I was once again sent out to catch the stupid dog.

This was Liza's plan, for me to go looking for the dumb dog, and just keep on going. I knew it would work because sometimes I spent the better part of 2 hours trying to catch that dog. It was now all set. I was personally guaranteed that Michelle would be ready to go at the drop of a dime. If she said for some reason that the car didn't work, again there was no way anyone would ever know what I had been planning my whole life.

Doorway to Freedom

The very next night the window/door of opportunity opened and I got my chance. I was never as scared in my entire life. I knew in my heart that I had to take this opportunity. With the kind of luck I had, the stupid dog would go out and get killed by a car, ruining all of my chances for freedom!

I couldn't call Liza or Michelle. I bundled up to go do my (almost) nightly duty, praying all the time that this last hope would not fail. We didn't even have payphones in our town, so I had to trust that what Liza had promised me was true. Remember this was before the cell phone!

I ran all the way to her door and knocked so hard I literally ripped the skin off my knuckles. Liza knew it was me. She was already dressed and had my pitiful bag of clothes in her hand. We didn't speak a word as we raced to Michelle's house for the great escape.

We were there before you knew it, but once again I was just waiting for problems to happen. Michelle wasn't ready. Every minute it took her to apply her makeup and fix her hair seemed like it took a lifetime.

Finally we were in the car and on the highway. I couldn't believe it. I felt like I was having the best dream of my life.

"Where are we going?" Michelle asked. This was not something I had given a lot of thought to. Not wanting to seem like a total idiot, I quickly told her to take me to my father's.

"Does he know you are coming?" was her next question.

I said, *"Yes"* even though I was filled with fear.

I remembered the last time I had called him to ask if I could go and live with him. His answer at that time was no for reasons I was and still am not sure of but I was past the point of caring I would live on the street if I had to now that I was on my way to freedom. It was too late now. I didn't care if I had to live in a cardboard box. I would not go back. I had come farther tonight to freedom than I had ever come in my life.

All too soon we were parked in front of my father's house. I really wasn't sure what I was going to do. Michelle was waiting for me to make a move. I was taking way too long. When she actually spoke, I almost jumped out of my skin, not realizing how quiet the car had got. Michelle was so nice.

"Do you want me to go in with you and tell them what's going on?" she asked.

This was something had to be done but I had to do it alone.

"No," I said, *"but could you wait here in case my father changed his mind?"*

Without hesitation, she said, *"Yes, of course."*

The steps loomed before me like a monster ready to swallow me up. I almost chickened out, but I knew I had to do it. I wasn't sure if I should knock or just go in. Every decision I had to make seemed incredibly difficult. I decided to knock just like a visitor and hope that I would be welcomed like a member of the family.

My father answered the door. I will never forget the look of shock on his face when he saw me standing there.

"Come in, come in." he said.

I don't think he knew what to expect. Before I knew what was happening, I blurted out, *"Can I stay here? Can I live with you?"* and I began to cry.

My stepmother, Marie didn't even hesitate to take me in her arms. For some reason, I felt like she understood, even though I hardly knew her. I felt like I was finally free. That, however, was not to be the case. It had nothing to do with my father or stepmother. The freedom I felt, I didn't get from going there. It took way too many years to realize it was me.

I know now that everything happens for a reason, even when we really don't understand what the reason is at the time. If I had carried out my plan of killing the people who made my life a living hell, God only knows where I would have ended up.

I thought in my innocence, that leaving the town I called *Hell* and the life I hated would solve all of my problems. The reality is, the problems were rooted deep inside of me by the time I had actually left my first home. I was a walking ball of hatred and anger. God help the people who crossed my path!

Life was not easy for anyone around me, especially those who tried to show me love. It took many years and many adventures, as I like to call them today, for me to truly understand this. But that's a whole other story. One that takes me... anywhere but here.

***

Pippi longstocking

She was a fictional character but she was also my hero. It started out as a series of children's books and adapted into multiple films and television series. 9-year-old Pippi is unconventional, assertive, and has superhuman strength, being able to lift her horse one-handed without difficulty. She frequently mocks and dupes adults she encounters, an attitude I myself felt I had adapted to survive life with mother. Pippi usually reserves her worst behavior for the most pompous and condescending of adults. Pippi's anger is reserved for the most extreme cases (whereas mine wasn't)., such as when a man ill-treats her horse. Like Peter Pan, Pippi does not want to grow up. She is the daughter of a buccaneer captain and as such has adventurous stories to tell. She has 4 best friends: two animals (her horse and a monkey) and two humans, the neighbor's children Tommy and Annika.

Company houses were used in the old war times to house the men and their families who came from far and wide to work the coal mines. This really meant anywhere outside of Nova Scotia. That seemed like a million miles away to us people who lived in the small coastal towns. They were built by the government and The old co-op store use to be the company store. It was a vicious circle of men working all week in the coal mines digging deep under the ground to keep the machinery running for the war. They worked all week charging what they needed at the company store and paying rent so the houses were never really theirs and poverty ran rampant. After the war the men dispersed with their families heading for the big cities like Montreal and Toronto. The remaining stayed on and bought out the company houses and worked the mines carrying on that way of life for many generations to come. Dying men being pulled from the underground on a weekly basis because of poor working conditions and gasses that no one really seemed to be worried about. The only worry was feeding your family and getting through the long cold winters.

www.ingramcontent.com/pod-product-compliance
Lightning Source LLC
Chambersburg PA
CBHW031841090426
42741CB00005B/317